WordPress for Beginners
A Simple Guide to Blogging for Profit

KEESHA METCALFE

ISBN:151975860X
ISBN-13:978-1519758606

DEDICATION

This book is dedicated to my former employers whose decision to let me go due to a merger was the best decision that they could have made. Had they not done so, I would not have discovered the wonderful world of blogging and the endless opportunities that it has afforded me. Many thanks.

CONTENTS

Acknowledgments   i

1   Introduction   8

2   My Story   11

3   Why you Should Become A Blogger   14

4   A Word About Blog Niches   19

5   How to Start A WordPress Blog   25

6   How To Post your First Blog Post   34

7   How To Add Pages to your Blog   38

8   Hosting   40

9   Essential Plugins   58

10   Monetizing your Blog   63

11 Get Ready to Make Profits from your Blog: A Checklist 80

12 How to Not Look Like A Newbie Blogger   95

13 How to Let Others Know About your Blog – Free Traffic 101

14 Glossary   107

15 Leave a Review on Amazon   189

16 About the Author   190

ACKNOWLEDGMENTS

I want to acknowledge God first and foremost for birthing the desire to blog in me. I was made to blog. I also want to acknowledge my husband and my two sons who have patiently endured as I worked on this project. I could not have done it without your help.

1 INTRODUCTION

Thanks to internet technology, anyone with a computer now has the opportunity to make money online. It seems as if everybody is starting an online business these days. And then there are others, like you, who want to start your own online business but don't know how to begin. You have no technical skills and you don't understand internet jargon. Yet deep down inside you have a passion for writing, you just aren't certain that you can make money online since you don't know the first thing about making money online, much less starting a blog. Deep down, you too want to be able to cash in on the vast number of internet earning opportunities but you are afraid. Afraid to fail. Afraid to look stupid. Afraid to start and not be able to pull it off. Does this describe you?

In this book I am going to show you exactly how YOU can start your very own WordPress blog without the need for any prior experience and without the need for technical skills. I will demonstrate to you in clear and simple terms how you too can earn a very decent income by starting your own blog as soon as you purchase this valuable book. *WordPress for Beginners: A Simple Guide to Blogging for Profit* will take you from where you are right now to becoming a competent and respected blogger with the ability to earn as much as 6 figures per year through blogging.

I now earn a full time income from blogging and online writing and when I started I knew absolutely nothing about blogging. I didn't even know what a blog was. All I knew was that I wanted to make money online. When I lost my corporate job as a Manager in a financial institution, I ventured into blogging, determined not to return to the corporate rat race. However, the process was arduous to say the least because I never understood all the jargon and I could not find a single resource that would outline the process in a simple and non-technical way. I wished there was a resource available that would make things simpler for me but I could find none. That is why I wrote this book. I know from my own personal experience how difficult it can be to start a blog without knowing anything about blogging. I know how difficult it can be to earn the first dollar as a blogger because I have gone through the process myself. I wrote this book to solve that problem for people like you and people like me; people who love to do things themselves and who want to make money online by blogging.

In this book you will learn everything from all the jargon involved in creating a WordPress blog to how to select a name for your blog to how to actually make money from your blog to mistakes to avoid during the process. It is all laid out in a way that will guarantee your success as a blogger. The tips and tricks that I will show you in this book will give you a clear advantage over others who are trying to make money online through blogging.

I promise you that if you follow the steps, the tips and advice outlined in this book, you will realize online success that you never dreamed was possible. The jumpstart that you will receive will give you the ability to earn a very good income through your blog in half the time that others do. You will become the envy of all your peers and you will be happy that you made the life changing decision to buy this book.

So what are you waiting for? RIGHT NOW is the perfect time to realize your dreams of making money online through blogging. The earlier you get started, the sooner you will be cashing in on this great income earning opportunity. So go ahead, click the "Buy Now" button and let's do this!

2 MY STORY

Today I earn a full time income through the internet. One of my favorite and better sources of online income is from blogging. If someone had told me a few years ago that I could earn a great living through blogging and without having to hold down a job at the same time, I would not have believed them. Fast forward 2 years down the road and that is exactly where I am. Living the lifestyle I have always wanted to live without all the drama that comes with running in the corporate rat race.

After becoming the victim of a merger and losing my job as a Manager at a financial institution, I had a hard time landing another job. The truth is though, that I was tired of the rat race and wanted to make money on my own terms. I wanted to become my own boss and to run my own show. But I didn't know where to start or how to start. I decided to try my luck at blogging. I had heard some stories of persons who had managed to make a good income for themselves by blogging and I wanted to try it for myself. So I set out and used WordPress to start my very first blog, all without any prior experience in this area. However, I was determined to succeed at this so I gave it everything I had. I tried to follow all instructions. I watched all the'how to' videos on Youtube that I could. I would teach myself this thing and I could not fail. The only problem was that I simply did not understand a lot of the terms and phrases and the jargon concerning blogging. I mean what exactly was a plugin? What was a landing page? Boy oh boy was I in over my head here! I hit a snag. What did all these terms mean?

I wished that I had a book that explained all the jargon and terms and phrases that I didn't understand. But there wasn't. I had to wade my way through all the information out there on the web to find out what these terms meant. Needless to say I spent several hours just wasting time trying to figure everything out. By this time I should have established my blog and started raking in some money but I hadn't because I just didn't get it. They say that anyone can start a blog so it should have been easier than this....surely. So I decided to write a book for all those wannabe bloggers who have stopped dead in their tracks on their mission to start a blog because they simply do not understand all the jargon behind it nor do they know how to use their blog to make money. This book includes a handy reference glossary for wannabe bloggers, new bloggers and not so new bloggers who may occasionally need to be reminded about what everything means. It also includes detailed information about the various ways you can earn money from your blog and what not to do in your blogging journey. You will thank me because I will save you valuable time and we all know that time is money right? Right! Absolutely right! So here we go. No more time to waste. There is money to be made out there folks! Let's get this over with so we can go make some dough!

3 WHY YOU SHOULD BECOME A BLOGGER

A Blog is a social media platform that allows the blogger to engage with others in cyberspace. Blog is the shortened form of the word weblog and it is similar to a website but unlike a website, is much more interactive and is focused on educating, informing or entertaining rather than on marketing a particular product or service. While a traditional website is simply a place where persons have the convenience of making online purchases or learning more about a particular company, product or service, a blog is all that and more. In addition to offering products or services, a blog contains information that is targeted to a specific audience without making a direct sales pitch. In several cases, the owner of the blog, or the blogger, interacts with their readers by creating and publishing blog posts or articles about a specific subject and allowing readers to comment, like or share their content with their friends and acquaintances online. It is similar to other online social media platforms like Facebook and Twitter but with added functionality and with total freedom to choose what topics to blog about. The blog is the property of the blogger (as long as it is self-hosted) unlike other social media platforms that are owned by the social network platform owners. So while you may have a Facebook account, Facebook has complete control over your account and may choose to shut it down if you violate any of their rules or for whatever other reason. The same thing applies to the other social media platforms including Twitter, Instagram, Pinterest, LinkedIn and all the other smaller social media platforms. With blogging, you are in control. You have the freedom to voice your opinions and to express yourself as you wish as long as you are not violating any legal or governmental rules and regulations.

Share Your Expertise and Earn on your terms

Are you an expert on a particular topic? You may have a talent that others would love to learn about; you may be a talented cook or you may have the ability to teach people about the stock market. Whatever your talent is, a blog can give you the outlet to share your expertise with the entire world. Thanks to the internet, unlike traditional media, you have access to global markets and are able to reach audiences that were not traditionally accessible to you. Not only can it be fulfilling to share your expertise with others, a blog also gives you the opportunity to earn unlimited income from that talent or area of expertise. While it does help if you also have a talent for writing and are able to write engaging and easily understandable content, it is not a pre-requisite for blogging success. Many successful bloggers blog about topics that they have gained years of experience with. For example, if you have worked as a computer technician, you could start a blog that teaches others exactly what you have learned through your years as a technician. If you are a stay at home mom, you could blog about your experience giving useful advice to other stay at home moms. The choices are endless.

Become a Thought Leader

Because blogging offers this opportunity for expression, you have the ability to become a thought leader in your area of expertise. Several bloggers are able to increase their ability to influence others through blogging. In addition, blogging could allow you to become an authority in your area of expertise. So if you are an author or a speaker or you simply want to increase your sphere of influence, blogging is an excellent vehicle for doing so. If you want to get noticed, start a blog. If you want to help people by sharing your knowledge, you have the potential to succeed as a blogger.

Let your Voice be Heard

Do you feel strongly about a particular topic? Are you passionate about it and want to share your views on the subject? Do you have something to say that could change someone's life for better? Do you long to share your point of view with anyone who will listen? If you find yourself nodding in agreement to these questions, then you should definitely start a blog. If you can express yourself well in writing and you want your voice to be heard, blogging can give you that voice. Some of us are more comfortable expressing ourselves in writing and don't want to be left out of the conversation simply because no one has given us the opportunity to speak or because we may feel uncomfortable expressing our strong views in person.

Everyone has something to say. Perhaps you have had a unique experience that you want to share with others. Maybe you want to document your struggles with a particular issue and how you overcame that challenge. This could very well encourage someone who may find himself or herself in a similar situation and who doesn't know how to handle it. Blogging affords you that outlet to express your opinions in written form. The written word is a beautiful thing and if you have a way with words, you may enjoy blogging tremendously. With a blog, the world is your stage and you are the main character. Express yourself!

4 A WORD ABOUT BLOG NICHES

If you hope to make a reasonable amount of income from your blog, it is important that you consider what niche you will focus on. A niche blog is a blog that focuses solely on a single subject or topic that has much depth but not much width. For example, you could create a niche blog about koi fish if that is the area you are passionate about and that blog that you create would be considered a niche blog. However, if you created a blog about fishes in general, that would not be considered a niche blog per se since the area of focus is so wide. In a way, all blogs focus on particular niches but the definition of a niche blog implies either a highly targeted audience or a highly targeted topic or both. As a blogger who wants to earn from blogging, it is advisable to focus on a very specific niche market.

In general, popular blog niches include fitness and dieting, personal finances, and relationships. The aim is to choose such a popular niche topic and to focus on a specific aspect of that topic or on a specific aspect of that market. For example, if you choose to start a health and wellness blog, you could select women over 40 as your niche market or if you choose to start a blog on personal finances, you could choose to focus on targeting single moms as your niche market. The niche market that you select must be one that has great potential for earning. You don't want to select a niche that is so highly competitive that your chances of succeeding are slim or a niche that has little competition but not enough interest for you to be able to generate a good income from it. To determine whether a particular niche has a lot of earning potential, you can conduct a Google keyword search. The aim is to find a topic that gets a huge amount of searches every month but that has a low level of competition. Such a topic has potential for great profitability. Here is how you would conduct a Google keyword search to find a potentially profitable blog topic. To use the Google keyword tool, you need to have a Google Adwords account.

Type in Google Adwords in your browser and click on the first result or simply type in https://www.google.com/adwords/ and press enter.

To create your account, just follow the instructions and provide the relevant answers. After you create your Google Adwords account, you will need to log in or sign in to your account.

Login > Tools and Analysis > Keyword Planner > Search for New Keyword and Ad Groups Ideas. The following menu should appear.

You should enter relevant information in at least one of the three boxes indicated at the top. Your product or service should be your targeted keywords (not broad single word keywords), your landing page should be either your home page or a specific landing page that you have created to collect leads and the product category should be your niche. After you have completed entering that information, you need to select your target market. Just select the main country where you will be targeting, the languages that you will be targeting, select Google search and type in any negative keywords that you don't want in your search results (although this is mainly aimed at Google Adwords customers). Next you should fill out the keyword filters section. This is where you will indicate the specific results that you need.

Click on the pencil where it says "keyword filters" and you will be taken to a new menu. The only options that apply are the average monthly searches and the competition level. Type in a figure that you don't want the average monthly searches to fall below. You should choose a relatively high figure that would indicate that the topic is highly researched on Google. Let's say you choose 5,000 monthly searches, you would type in 5,000 in the relevant box. Next you should select "low" competition. Where it says "keyword options" you should select "on" to show only ideas that are closely related to key terms. Where it says "keywords to include" you can enter any appropriate information. Click on get ideas to see your results.

You should see a list of keyword ideas that have great profitability potential – good level of monthly searches plus a low level of competition.

You can then use the Google Trends tool to find out whether your intended niche is declining or increasing in interest. Those that are increasing or that show a good level of stability are the ones that you should focus on.

Find Google Trends at https://www.google.com/trends. Then you should type in the keywords ideas that you found using the keyword planner and press enter. You should look for a graph that shows a growing trend. Once you find a graph that is trending upwards and indicates a growing or stable interest, you have found a potentially profitable niche.

You may opt to use one or more of these result options as the main keywords that you want your blog to rank for on Google. You may use these keywords in your domain name or in your site tag line for search engine optimization purposes.

You can use the Google keyword planner to also get ideas for blog posts. It is a very useful tool that you should take full advantage of.

5 HOW TO START A WORDPRESS BLOG

Starting a WordPress blog is a relatively simple exercise, even for persons without any programming or technical computer skills. However, if you don't know the jargon, it can be confusing and frustrating.

WordPress is a Content Management System (CMS) that allows you to create your very own online blog for free. There is no need to worry about hosting costs or paying to register a domain name unless you choose to run a self-hosted blog. Running a self-hosted blog is my recommendation if you want to make profits from your blog, but it is not mandatory. You can still make profit from a free WordPress blog. However, there will be limitations which I will explain in the next chapter. For now, I will demonstrate how to set up your blog on Wordpress.

How to Set Up Your Account on WordPress

In order to set up your WordPress account you need to go to WordPress.com and click on Create a Website. First you need to register for an account on Wordpress. Here are the steps:

www.wordpress.com > Create Website > Login > Register

You will need to enter your email address, choose a username and a password as well as decide on a name for your blog. If you are signing up for a free account your blog name will have the dot wordpress dot com extension. Click on Register or Sign up when you've finished entering all the required details.

Quick Tip: Be sure to choose a name that contains the main keywords that you would like your blog to rank for. This makes it easier for your blog to show up in search engine queries that include your keyword. In other words, this makes for great SEO (search engine optimization) and gives you an easy way to bring lots of free traffic to your website.

When you have completed registration, you will be sent an email for you to confirm your account. Simply click on the link that you receive in the email and that will confirm your account registration. This will bring you to your Dashboard which is your administration panel. You should see the message "Welcome to WordPress.com!" Here is where you will do all of the posting and the management of your new blog.

This is what your dashboard should look like. Take note of the big red arrow on the right. You should click on each of those links to write a post, set up your general settings, create your profile, select a theme for your blog, upgrade your blog if you want greater functionality and added options. You can also learn more about Wordpress by clicking on Wordpress.tv.

Subscribe To Gravatar and Create a Profile

I would suggest that the first thing that you do is set up your profile. Here is where you will set up your gravatar account or your online public profile. Simply click on the link that says "Your Profile". Then enter the required information as outlined in the following paragraph.

Once you have set up a Wordpress account on WordPress.com, you have the option of creating a Gravatar. A Gravatar (Globally Recognized Avatar) is essentially a service that allows you to create an avatar that will be used as your online 'ID'. You are able to upload a photograph of yourself to be used as your online profile as well as the ability to provide links to your blog, website and/or social media accounts. Your gravatar picture will appear anywhere in the blogosphere that you post a comment on a blog or a website. When persons use their mouse to hover over your gravatar, they may be able to view the information that you included in your description when you created your gravatar account if you enable that feature in your profile settings. If someone clicks on your gravatar, they will be able to see your full profile which may include a photograph of yourself, your description, links to your blog or website etc. A gravatar is a very useful way of introducing yourself online and for getting persons to find out more about you and what you have to offer. In other words, this is an excellent marketing tool and you should make full use of it. Ensure that your description paints you in a positive light and that it tells readers what your blog is about and that it gives readers a compelling reason to want to visit your blog. Here is what default gravatars look like:

If you have uploaded a photograph, it will appear on your gravatar instead of a default gravatar and may look like one of these:

What is a gravatar?

A gravatar, or globally recognized avatar, is quite simply an avatar image that follows you from weblog to weblog appearing beside your name when you comment on gravatar enabled sites. Avatars help identify your posts on web forums, so why not on weblogs?

General Settings

After creating your profile, you should then endeavour to set up your General Settings. Click on the General Settings in the Dashboard Tab.

Here you will enter information such as your Site title, your tag line, your timezone, date format, time format, and your language. Remember to include your main keywords in both your Site title and your tag line. Save the changes and then you can go to Settings in the Dashboard (on the left) and Select the different subheadings to change them to your liking. Apart from "General", the other subheadings are:

Writing

Reading

Discussion

Media

Sharing

Polls

AdControl

Email Post Changes

OpenId and

Webhooks.

Select Your Theme

Then it's time to select your theme. There are several Wordpress themes available for you to choose from. You should select one that is suitable for both you and your audience. You can select a free theme or a premium (paid) theme. While there are some excellent free themes available, they do have limited functionality and fewer customization options. To maximize your blogging experience, I recommend that you select a premium theme. There are compelling reasons why you should consider upgrading to a premium WordPress theme although there are some great free themes available. Some of the reasons for selecting a premium theme include increased ability to customize your blog to give it the look and the feel that you want. In addition, premium themes are normally responsive (easily viewed from mobile devices). Responsiveness is now a factor that Google takes into consideration when determining page rank so it is important that you select a theme that is responsive. The developers of premium themes also usually offer personalized email support so that you can contact them directly if you ever have any problems with your theme. As a beginner, it is very possible that there will be issues that you will face with your theme for which you will need assistance. Free themes usually only offer forum support and you are not guaranteed an answer or a solution to your questions or concerns. Premium theme develops normally offer email support for individual customers. Browser compatibility is also something that usually comes with the premium theme packages. It is important that your theme supports the most popular browsers such as Google Chrome, Mozilla Firefox or Internet Explorer. By ensuring that your theme supports several different browsers, you are ensuring that potential readers and potential customers are able to read your blog without any issues. If you plan to advertise on your blog, you also need to look for a theme that offers sidebar and widget options where you can place your ads, affiliate links etc.

Once you have selected, installed and customized your theme, you should be ready to post your first blog post!

6 HOW TO POST YOUR FIRST BLOG POST

Here is where it gets exciting. To set up your first blog post, go to your dashboard. In your dashboard, click on Posts > Add New.

You will be taken to a screen that looks like this:

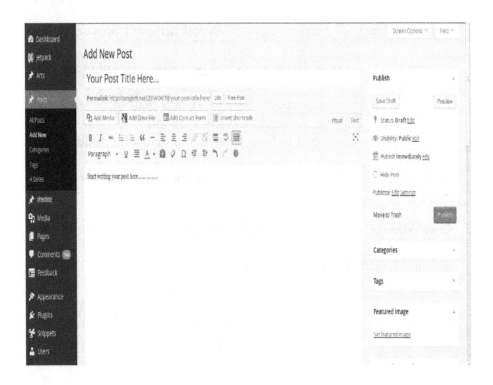

The cursor should be flashing where it says "Your Post Title Here". Go ahead and type in the title that you want to give to your new post. Then click in the blank area beneath that to enter your blog post. The toolbar directly above the post area allows you to format your post to give it the look and feel that you want it to. From here you can also add images and videos and other types of media to enhance your blog posts. As you type, be certain to click

"Save Draft" in the upper right hand corner periodically to save your work.

Categories

Click the down arrow next to categories to add categories to your blog. Categories allow you to help your users to easily find information on your blog. For example, let's say you are creating a food blog. Your categories may be Breakfast, Lunch, Dinner, Snacks etc. Select an appropriate category for your post and enter it.

Tags

Enter tags for your post. Tags are words that will tell readers at a glance what your post is about. These also help with search engine optimization and help others to find your information easily on the web. Let's say you are posting an omelette recipe. Appropriate tags may be recipes, omelette, breakfast, eggs etc.

Featured Images

If you want to include an image on your post, you may click the featured image link and it will ask that you upload an image. Go ahead and upload an image from your computer or from elsewhere.

When you are through entering the appropriate category, tags and an appropriate image, click on "save draft". You may preview the post by clicking the "Preview" button. As soon as you are satisfied that everything is okay, you may go ahead and click "Publish". Congratulations, your first post is now live and available on the worldwide web!

7 HOW TO ADD PAGES TO YOUR BLOG

Now that you have created your first blog post, it's time to add some pages to your blog. The first page that you should consider adding is the "About" page.

The steps for adding a new "About" page are as follows:

Page > Add New > Click in the Title Bar and type in the word "About" > Click in the body area and enter your description. Your "About" page is a very important page on your blog. It should give your reader some background about you as an individual or as a business. The intention is to introduce yourself to your readers and to give them a reason to take you seriously. A good about page gives you the opportunity to convert visitors into subscribers and/or customers. This is where you get the chance to show your visitors how you can help them and how your products, services or how the information that you divulge can benefit them. Essentially your about page is where you get to make your elevator pitch. It should answer the questions about who are you, what you have to offer, why visitors should use your site, when you started doing what you are doing, how you can help them and why they should read and subscribe to your blog. It's as simple as that but many bloggers fail to do it right. Also, be certain to upload a photograph (a head shot is sufficient) of yourself to give your blog a face and a personality. To do this, simply click on the "Add Media" button, select the file that you want to upload and insert it into the post. People like to know the face behind the blog and are more likely to view you as a real person who cares about their needs if you include a professional picture on your "About" profile.

You should also add a "Contact" page where you will include information about how users may reach you such as your email address, your telephone numbers, your social media pages and your physical address (if applicable).

Add as many pages as you deem appropriate for your blog by repeating the steps previously outlined.

8 HOSTING

WordPress will host your website for you for free. However, as long as you have a free WordPress account, your domain name will always include the wordpress.com extension. However, it is possible to get a professional domain name (without the WordPress extension) without self-hosting. WordPress gives you the option of purchasing your own domain main (for about $18 per annum) while still being hosted by WordPress.com. So you will have a professional domain name, which gives the appearance that you are self-hosted, but you're really being hosted by WordPress. The only drawback with this is that you won't be able to use any plugins or to advertise on your blog. This is my recommended choice for the first 3 months as a newbie blogger. It gives you the opportunity to give a professional image without having to pay for hosting as well as the safety of the WordPress.com platform.

However, if you will be blogging for profit, it is essential that you eventually upgrade to a self-hosted blog. This will allow you to add advertisements to your blog so you can monetize it and earn maximum income from your blogging efforts.

When to Self-Host Your Blog

There are some who would recommend that as soon as you start your WordPress blog that you should seek to have it independently hosted by a webhost such as Bluehost, Go Daddy or Host Gator. *However, based on my own experience, my recommendation would be to delay self-hosting at least for the first 3 or so months.* I have started several different blogs using either of these ways –

starting with Wordpress and then self-hosting after 3 months as well as self-hosting immediately. The former method worked much better for me and I am confident that it will work better for you as well. I say this because those first 3 months allowed me to really focus on building a following and on learning the ropes of blogging first without worrying too much about monetization and earning. It also allowed me to learn from my mistakes so that when I was ready to monetize and to open my blog up to the entire blogosphere that I knew what I was doing and that I gave a professional impression. I like to think of this period before self-hosting as a type of incubation period for your blog. This is necessary in order that you can build a community and a following before going off on your own and self-hosting.

Research has shown that many bloggers quit after the first 3 months when they don't see the results that they want to see. I don't want you to be among those statistics. That is why I have written this book – to help to make you a success and not a failure. And that is why I am strongly recommending that you don't self-host immediately. Many new bloggers get frustrated because they expect it to be an easy process where they just set up a blog, put out some content, and sit back expecting to get a huge following and to make a killing with minimal, inconsistent effort. The truth is, it doesn't work that way. Becoming a successful blogger requires hard work, dedication and consistency. It is not going to happen overnight.

Allowing WordPress to host your account for free in the first few months has the advantage of allowing you access to a huge community of bloggers with whom you can connect, collaborate and build a solid online presence. Fellow bloggers are more likely to support your online efforts and are more likely to interact with you online than non-bloggers. While fellow bloggers may not be your target market, they are a valuable resource for new ideas, collaboration and support; especially in those initial months when you are just learning. In those first few months, you want to spend the time following and connecting with other bloggers in similar niches and learning from them. In turn, some of them will follow your blog and they will become your first source of free traffic. This helps to build your online confidence and serves as a learning ground for you. In addition, while you are getting this free traffic, it will help to improve your Alexa ranking (see glossary for further details) as well as the chances that your blog will appear in search engine keyword searches. In other words, you will spend the time giving yourself a jump start so that you maximize your chances of earning when you actually begin to monetize your blog.

Please note that during this incubation period, you should still write your blog articles with your target audience in mind. It must be mentioned that many new bloggers note a marked difference in community engagement whenever they upgrade from WordPress.com hosting to self-hosting (WordPress.org). This is because WordPress.com does not allow self-hosted bloggers easy access to the blogging community and WordPress.org (the self-hosted version of the WordPress Content Management System) has a much less engaged and interactive community of bloggers. It is natural to feel like a fish out of water once you leave the comfort of the WordPress.com community and venture out on your own by self-hosting. It is a bit like leaving home for the first time. You may feel a little lonely and a little isolated. But don't despair. The time you spend "in the incubator" will prepare you adequately for succeeding in the 'real' blogosphere.

While it may be tempting to remain in the comforts of the WordPress.com community, you must eventually self-host to maximize your income-generating efforts from blogging. So as soon as those first 3 months have passed, be certain to upgrade to self-hosting.

N.B: If you choose to forego the incubation period, the first thing that you should do is purchase a domain name and then seek hosting.

Hosting – Selecting a Host

Having learned and grown during the incubation period, it is now time to migrate your blog to WordPress.org and self-host. First you would need to decide upon which host to use. I personally use Bluehost for all my blogs because I believe that they offer the best service. They have also been around since 1996 and have a great deal of experience and expertise. Bluehost is also recommended by WordPress. I have tried signing up with Go Daddy but they make the process very technical and involved in my opinion. I could do without all that technicality. However, there are some bloggers who are happy with their experience using Go Daddy. In any case, you need to do your own research where selecting a host is concerned. Some popular hosts are Bluehost, Go Daddy, Host Gator, In Motion, Web Hosting Hub, and Site Ground. You want to select a host that is reliable and one that has great customer reviews. Cost should also be taken into consideration as this can vary widely between hosts. Simply do a Google search on the different hosts to find out as much as you can about each one.

Some of the perks of self-hosting include getting a more professional look, the ability to advertise, the ability to add plugins to increase functionality and the ability to establish several email addresses using your new domain name as the ending (instead of @yahoo or @gmail or @hotmail.com).

As soon as you have decided upon a host, you will need to purchase a domain name as well as purchase hosting for your blog. Whatever host you decide to go with, you should visit that website and purchase your domain name as well as sign up for hosting. Hosting is simply the process of making your blog 'live' and available for others to view on an ongoing basis. It is similar to having a cable subscription where you pay to be able to view certain channels for a certain period of time. Similarly, when you pay for hosting, you are really paying to make your blog accessible to others on the internet on an ongoing basis.

Selecting a Domain Name for Your Blog

You may decide to continue to use the domain name that you purchased during your 3 months incubation period or if you didn't choose to do that, you will need to purchase a new domain name.

The domain name that you select for your blog is very important for SEO and other reasons. If you are satisfied with the root name that you had chosen for your WordPress.com blog, you can maintain that name without the dot wordpress extension. If not, you can opt to purchase a brand new domain name. Here are some tips for selecting the ideal domain name:

Include your main keywords in your domain name. For example, if your blog is a fashion blog, it may be very helpful to use the word "fashion" as a part of your domain name. That way, your blog is more likely to appear in searches with the keyword "fashion". If you are going to be blogging for profit, it is critical that people be able to find you through keyword searches. There is a great market out there available to you but if your blog is not appearing in search engine searches, you are at a great disadvantage. So please pay maximum attention to this when naming your blog. This is not to say that if you don't include keywords that people will not be able to find you through keyword searches. They very well may find you but you will have to work harder to get noticed. Those blogs that have keywords in their domain names are more likely to appear on the first 2 pages of Google keyword search results. This is important information because studies have shown that 94% of online purchasing done following a keyword search, are from websites that appear on page 1 in the search engines. Page 2 blogs or websites take the remaining 6%. So the aim is to be able to rank on the first page two pages for your particular keywords.

Next, your **domain name should reflect your blog focus topic**. Persons should not have to guess what your blog is about. It should be immediately obvious what your main focus is. My advice is also to not use your own name alone as a domain name unless you are already famous or already have celebrity status. So while you may want to get your name out there, if you are not yet quite in the league of Oprah Winfrey or Tom Cruise, for SEO purposes, it may be better to use a more appropriate name for your blog. Think about it this way. If you are a fashion blogger and you name your blog Kellystevens.com, persons that need fashion advice but who don't know who you are or what you do, are very unlikely to click on your URL. On the other hand if your domain name was something like KellysFashionSchool.com, that may be a more appropriate domain name that would attract a higher click through rate when someone does a keyword search with the word "fashion" included.

When selecting a domain name, it is also important that you **select a name that offers a wide scope** and that will not be so narrow that you are limited in what you can write about on the topic. This is not to say that you shouldn't focus on a niche. It just means that you should leave room for expansion of your main topic if the need arises in the future. For example, it would be better to use the domain name cookingwithcathy.com rather than the domain name cookingchickenwithcathy.com. This way, if you want to expand your focus outside of cooking chicken, there will be no issues since the domain name would easily allow you to do so.

While your domain name may have different extensions such as .com or .co or .org or .edu or .net etc, dot com is by far the most popular option. Dot org is usually used by non-profit or governmental organizations while dot edu is normally used to indicate an educational organization such as a school or other learning institution. As a newbie blogger, I suggest that your best bet would be to stick with .com and if you have the funds to do so, you may also purchase the .net extension. Also, some countries such as the UK and Canada offer the .uk or the .ca extensions so that users can easily tell where the blog is based. The choice is yours whether to use country extensions or not. If you are only marketing in that country then having a country extension may be a good idea. If not, you may not want to limit yourself.

You may also use hyphens to separate different words in your domain name but these are usually harder for people to remember. My advice would be to stick with domains without the hyphen if the intent is to have a memorable domain name that people can easily recall.

In summary, use a domain name that is SEO friendly, reflective of your blog focus, offers scope for expansion and that is memorable.

How to Upgrade and Migrate from WordPress.com to Self-hosting

Once you have selected and purchased your domain name, it is time to migrate your blog over to your host's servers. (***Skip the following steps if you had decided to self-host immediately***). But first you want to install a 301 redirect plugin on your old blog or website. The reason for installing this plugin is to avoid people getting 404 error messages when they click on links to your original blog. A 404 error message is a message that tells the user that the page that they are looking for no longer exists. You want to get this plugin so that if anyone clicks on your old blog URLs, they will be automatically redirected to your new blog without getting an error message. Another reason for using this plugin is to avoid getting penalized by Google. If users are constantly getting

404 errors, Google will drop your rank and this will definitely affect you negatively where search engine traffic is concerned. To preserve your ranking, you need to install this plugin on your original blog before migration. Here is how to do it.

Plugins >Add New >Type '301 redirect' > Click Download or Install > Activate Plugin

As soon as you have done this, you need to type in the source and the destination URLs by following these steps: From the dashboard, click on

Tools > Redirection > type in the source URL (address for your existing blog) and type in the destination URL (address for new blog) > Add Redirection

Now you need to save all the information from your old blog so that you can export it over to your new blog home. You will have to create the export file:

Tools > Export (click to export XML file) > Select All Content > Download Export File

The file will be saved in your downloads folder or wherever you specify for it to be saved.

Now you need to export this file to your new blog.

Open another tab on your computer and type in the URL for your host account (This example is for those using Bluehost.com). For other hosts just follow the step by step directions. Log into your account and you should land on the hosting tab (after you get rid of all the irrelevant pop ups)

Step 1

Search for and click on

Install Wordpress > Install > Select the latest version of Wordpress > Select the relevant domain (the new domain name that you had purchased).

Step 2

Give your new blog a site name which should be the same as the domain name that you purchased but without the www and without the dot com extension. Also, change your login details. This is where you select a username and a password for your new blog. You will use this each time you need to log into your blog. You can skip step 3 and go on to Step 4 where you will read the terms and conditions, agree to them and then click on 'complete' when you are done.

You should then log into your new blog site using the username and password that you just created. If your domain name was www.mynewblog.com, you should type in www.mynewblog.com/wp-admin to go to your log in page.

This is what the login page should look like:

Once you log into your account, you should end up on your dashboard. Now it's time to import all the files from your original blog over to your new blog. From the dashboard of your new blog, click on

Tools > Import > Select Wordpress > Choose File (select the XML file that you had originally exported and saved) > Upload File and Import

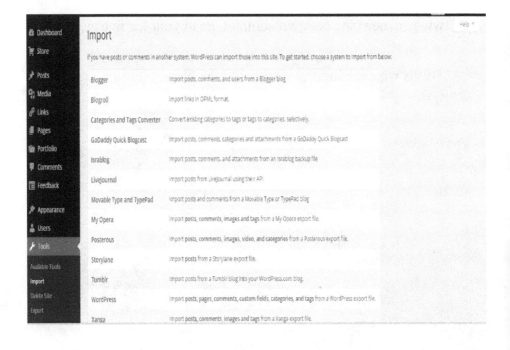

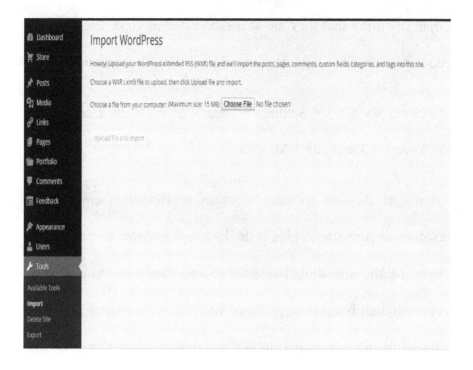

When your files have been exported, you should click on the Posts tab to verify that all your files have been uploaded from your previous blog. In addition, you need to delete the "Hello World" post that comes with the WordPress template. To do this go to the dashboard:

Posts > All Posts > Look for Hello World > Hover the Mouse Button over it and then click "trash".

Migrate Your Subscribers

If you originally had subscribers to your WordPress.com blog, you want to ensure that they are still subscribed to your new blog. To do this you need to log into your original WordPress account.

Click on My Sites > Settings > Jetpack Status > click on migrate followers > Select site > Migrate

That's it! Be sure to also select an appropriate theme and to customize your site to give it the look and feel that you want it to have. Ideally you should select the same theme that you used on your original blog. If not, ensure you select a theme that at least has all the features that your last theme had. All this can be done from the dashboard by selecting the Appearance tab > Themes and Appearance > Customize

9 ESSENTIAL PLUGINS

Plugins are great ways to add functionality to your new blog. There are several plugins available from you to choose from but I want to give you my recommendations for must-have plugins that I believe that every profit blogger should have. To activate each plugin, go to your dashboard:

Plugins > Add New > Type plugin name in search box > Download and Install > Activate Plugin. Please note that all these plugins are free to download.

Now, here are my recommended plugins for your blog: You may also research other plugins for yourself but based on my own experience, these are the ones that I recommend.

1. **Jetpack** - I am strongly recommending that you activate Jetpack on your blog. It is a robust, highly useful 'plugin' that will allow you to add widgets to your blog so that you can display ads, display social media dashboards such as Facebook, Twitter, Pinterest and Google Plus as well as several other options. The features of the Jetpack plugin

include customization, mobile themes, content tools, visitor engagement tools, site performance tools, and security tools.

2. **WordPress SEO by Yoast** – As the name suggests, this plugin is very helpful in helping you to optimize your content for search engines. It keeps your writing focused by encouraging you to select a keyword for each blog post and to include vital SEO elements such as including keywords in the title of each post etc. This is a free plugin that also creates an XML sitemap for you. This XML sitemap allows Google and other search engines to be better able to crawl your website or blog so that your posts appear in keyword search results. This plugin has been a great help for me and has allowed me to rank on the first few pages of Google for some keywords.

3. **Contact Form 7** – This plugin allows you to easily create contact forms within your content to allow persons to be able to send you a message directly from your blog. You can easily customize the form to fit your needs and tastes.

4. **Google Analytics Dashboard for WP** – Every blogger who is serious about making money blogging must install this plugin. However, you must have your Google Analytics account set up before you can install this plugin. To do this type in Google Analytics in your browser (https://www.google.com/analytics/) and set up your account. Simply follow the step by step instructions.

This plugin will allow you to easily monitor and track all the activity that takes place on your blog including the number of visitors that you receive, how long they spend on your site and what posts or pages they are reading on your blog. A report is produced that you can easily view from your dashboard. Google Analytics plugin can help you to improve the performance of your blog when used in conjunction with your full Google Analytics report that you will get from your Google Analytics account.

5. **A Backup plugin** – Like the name suggests, a backup plugin will automatically back up your website or blog for you based on the schedule that you select when you set it

up on your blog. This is essential since you would not want to lose any of the information that you have on your blog. Whenever the host servers are being maintained or whenever you conduct certain types of activities such as changing your theme or if you unfortunately happen to have your website hacked etc, there is a possibility that you could lose some information. In order to make it automatic and so that you don't always have to remember to back up your blog, you should install a backup plugin. Some of the best WordPress backup plugins are Vault Press (paid), Backup Buddy (paid), BackWPup (free), BackUpWordPress (free), Updraft Plus (free), Duplicator (free), WP-DB-Backup (free). Choose an appropriate one based on your personal preferences.

These are the plugins that you absolutely must have if you are blogging for profit. There are several others that you may choose to install along your blog journey. Just don't go overboard with plugins because some of them are incompatible with others and may crash your blog. Also, the more plugins you have on your blog, the longer your site takes to load which affects your bounce

rate and may result in fewer conversions.

10 MONETIZING YOUR BLOG

Congratulations! It is now time to learn how to make money from your blog. While there are several different ways that you can make money from your blog, I am going to tell you about the most popular ways to monetize your site. The first way is through affiliate marketing.

Affiliate Marketing

Many bloggers choose to monetize through Affiliate marketing. This is where the blogger partners with an affiliate to make sales on the affiliate's behalf or to send leads to the affiliate's website. As an affiliate marketer, you make a commission each time someone purchases an affiliate's products or services through your website. When you sign up as an affiliate, you will receive a unique code that will be used by the affiliate partner to track and identify any sales that are made through customers that click on your website and who eventually end up making a purchase. Normally, the affiliate partner would provide you with different types of links that you can display on your website in strategic locations to attract the attention of persons browsing on your blog. The most common types of links include banners and text links. Banners come in the form of an image with an attached code that includes your unique affiliate ID. When someone clicks on the banner, they are normally taken to the affiliate's website where they will find further information about the product or service being advertised, and they will be given the opportunity to make a purchase. Many bloggers use their side bars or header to display affiliate banners. Text links are normally integrated into blog posts through hyperlinking. You can recognize the hyperlink in the toolbar of your post section by looking for a small chain link.

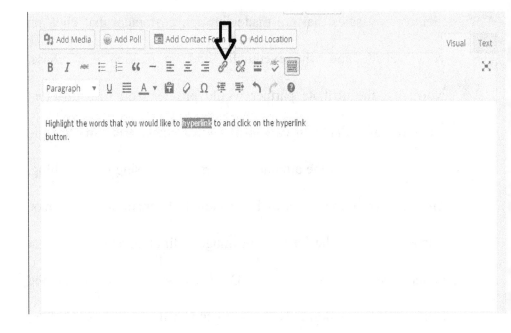

Highlight the words that you would like to hyperlink to and click on the hyperlink button.

Once you click on the hyperlink icon, you will be directed to a screen to put in the link URL which is the affiliate text link that you received from your affiliate partner. You should paste it into the URL box, click "open in a new window' and click 'Add link' at the bottom of the screen.

Insert/edit link   ✕

Enter the destination URL

URL [   ]

Title [   ]

☐ Open link in a new window/tab

Or link to existing content ▲

Search [   ]

No search term specified. Showing recent items.

When visitors click on the hyperlinked text, they will be taken to the affiliate's website and given the opportunity to make a purchase.

There are several affiliate marketing opportunities available. However, there are several that are not completely honest in their dealings. I have personally been ripped off by affiliate partners who had no intention of ever paying any commission on the sales that were generated through my website. Even though their analytical reports indicated that sales had been generated through my blog, I never received any commission for those sales. In addition, when I contacted them about it, they failed to address the issue. I eventually opted out of that program because I was not about to make somebody else rich and not receive any compensation for my efforts. I say this to emphasize the point that you should be very careful which affiliate programs you sign up for. Do your research before signing up and speak with other affiliates about their experiences before deciding to enrol in an affiliate program.

You want to choose reputable affiliate marketing networks like Share A Sale (http://www.shareasale.com) which allows you to apply to become an affiliate for several different, reputable affiliate partners. Amazon Associates also has a very popular affiliate program that allows you to make affiliate sales from many of the products that are sold through Amazon. However, as with all affiliate programs, in order to make a good amount of earnings, you need to have a lot of traffic coming to your blog or website. Also, the commissions are not very high but it is still a very viable option if you can make several sales per period.

Clickbank also offers several different affiliate products that you can choose from, but they specialize in digital products (such as

PDF books) that can be downloaded upon purchase. You can earn up to 75% commission as a Clickbank affiliate. You must do your own research to ascertain which products are more likely to sell on your blog and which partners are suitable for you. It is best to look for products that your particular blog audience may be interested in buying. For example, if you have a health blog, it may be good to market a workout plan or a health and fitness ebook to your blog readers. Just ensure that the product is relevant and try to avoid marketing a product just because it is popular. If it has no relevance to your audience, you are unlikely to make any sales. Clickbank also gives you the opportunity to sell your own digital affiliate products and to get affiliates to market these on your behalf.

It should be noted and is worth repeating that in order to do well with affiliate marketing, you need to have quite a bit of traffic coming to your blog. This will greatly increase the likelihood that someone will click on one of your affiliate links and make a purchase. Most affiliate programs use cookies to track user activity so that if a user on your blog clicks on an affiliate link on your site but doesn't make a purchase right away, that cookie will allow the user to be tracked for as many as 180 days after clicking. If a purchase is made within the applicable 180 day window, the purchase would be linked to your affiliate ID and you should be credited for the purchase. You should consider how long each affiliate partner stores cookies. It normally ranges from 30 to 180 days. The longer the time frame, the greater your chances of earning a sales commission.

Affiliate marketing is also very competitive since several bloggers use this means to monetize their blogs. Only those bloggers who are able to generate good amounts of traffic and who are strategic in their affiliate marketing make any significant money through this process. The key is to not only create banner ads as the sole strategy for driving sales, but to actively blog about the various products or services and to do other activities to build awareness and to encourage purchases. This must be carried out on an ongoing and consistent basis.

Most affiliate programs are free and require no money for enrolment.

Google Adsense

Google Adsense is a free program offered by Google that allows you to advertise targeted products and services on your blog next to your content. You have very likely seen these ads when you visit different blogs or websites and may wonder how it is that certain ads seem to appear on every single website of blog that you visit. These are Google Adsense ads that advertisers pay Google to display on blogs or websites. They are highly targeted based on your location, your blog niche and on the browsing habits of blog visitors.

With this program, as a blogger, Google provides you with an ad code that you will paste on your website or blog in areas on your site where you want the ads to appear. Advertisers place bids in order to be able to advertise on your website and the highest paying bidders get the opportunity to have their ads displayed on your blog or website. Google in turn pays you when visitors click on these ads. Google offers you the option of blocking ads that you don't feel are appropriate or relevant to your blog. You will also be able to view analytics which will indicate to you how hard your blog is working on your behalf. This is a great option for earning passive income from your blog. However, like affiliate marketing, you need to be able to generate lots of traffic to your blog in order to make a reasonable amount of income from these Google Adsense ads.

Importantly, if you have just started blogging, it is unlikely that Google will approve your Google Adsense application. You need to have a good amount of content on your site and your blog needs to be at least 6 months old before you should reasonably expect to be approved for this type of monetization. In addition, your content must be of good quality before Google will allow you to earn through ads. With that said, Google Adsense is a good earning option if you have some experience under your belt as a blogger and you should wait at least 6 months before applying for the Google Adsense ad program. Make this a goal of yours and work hard during the first 6 months of setting up your blog to build a following and to populate your website with high quality content.

Marketing your own Products or Services

Every blogger can earn money by marketing their own products or services through their blog. This is personally my preferred method of earning income from blogging. This is because I get 100% of the income that I make using this method of monetization. Also, there is much less competition when compared to affiliate marketing since my product or service would be unique to me. When a blogger sells affiliate products or services, they are usually selling a product or service that any other blogger in the same niche is possibly marketing as well. However, with your own product or service, you are selling something that is different and that you get all the credit for. Again, the product or service that you choose should be relevant to your blog and to your blog audience. Many bloggers choose to create things such as E-books and market these from their blogs. The contents of the ebook should be something that your readers would be interested in reading. You can also sell other products that you make or manufacture for yourself. For example if you blog about hair and you make hair products, you can sell those hair products through your blog. You can collect payments by setting up shopping carts on your blog so that you can easily process payments. Sometimes this is as simple as installing an ecommerce plugin that will allow you to sell your products through your blog. However, some plugins necessitate that you must have an ecommerce theme in order to get the best experience with these ecommerce plugins. Some of the most popular ecommerce plugins are:

Woocommerce which is courtesy of Wordpress.org. It has several different features including allowing you to collect payments through Paypal. You don't need to have an ecommerce theme to use this plugin.

WP E-commerce which is also very popular.

iThemes Exchange: Simple Ecommerce which is a highly rated plugin developed by iThemes. This plugin may be used to sell digital products as well as physical products from your blog.

Cart66 Lite: WordPress Ecommerce also allows you to sell both digital and physical products.

Jigoshop has a high user rating and is a great ecommerce plugin.

You can also market your services through your website. For example, if you are a freelance writer, you can advertise your services on your blog and have people order your services directly from your blog or website. Many authors also choose to market their books through their blogs while keeping their readers updated on new books in the pipeline. Whatever the product or service, it is possible to market it through your blog. The beauty about marketing through your blog is that you have the ability to reach a very wide market that may not be readily accessible to you if you set up a brick and mortar operation.

You are also able to sell services such as online courses through your blog. These may be done through email marketing or through webinars or through other learning management systems.

Selling Products Using the Drop Shipping Model

You can also sell products using the dropshipping model. With this model, you can buy products individually from a wholesaler and have them shipped directly to a retailer. As a blogger, you can partner with a dropshipping supplier and list their products for sale on your website or blog. When someone orders through your blog, you place the order with your drop shipping partner and they process the order and send it directly from their own warehouse directly to the retail customer. You would receive a commission based on the profits realized from the sale. Commissions vary widely from as low as 5% to as much as 100%. This is a viable option especially if you do not want the hassle of handling inventory or having to worry about shipping and handling. However, it is important that you choose a good drop shipping partner since any mess ups that they may make such as delayed shipping or sending the wrong product, may be blamed on you since the order originated through your website. With that said, be prepared to do thorough research when selecting a drop shipping partner.

Paid Memberships and Subscriptions

While this is not a popular method of monetization, it is a great way to earn income from your blog. Some bloggers will only allow paying members access to certain parts of their content. This method of monetization is a great option if you want to build your online community while earning from your expertise. Any blogger who has expertise in a particular area can set up a paid membership area on their blog. This is especially true if you have a highly desirable skill that readers would be willing to pay to learn more about. If for example, you blog about personal finances and you are knowledgeable about how to trade on the stock market, you could probably offer stock trading tips and advice to paid members on your blog. While some of your content would remain free, by adding a paid membership option, you can take advantage of the opportunity to earn from your skills and talents.

Setting up paid membership on your blog can be as simple as installing a plugin that will allow you to do so. Some things to consider when selecting a paid membership WordPress plugin include ease of use, the learning curve, how charges are prorated, payment gateway options, sequential delivery, one-click upsells and downsells etc. While there are several paid membership plugins available, it may be worth checking out these suggestions:

1. Cart66 Cloud

2. iThemes Exchange Membership Add-On

3. PMPro Woocommerce

4. MemberPress

5. MagicMembers

All these plugins have several features and I am deliberately refraining from recommending any particular one. This is because it really depends on the type of membership program that you would offer. The plugin that you choose should be based on your specific needs and desires.

Sponsored Banner Ads and Sponsored Posts

If your blog gets to the point where you have a good amount of highly targeted traffic and you have become somewhat of an authority within your particular niche, there may be some businesses that are willing to pay to advertise on your blog. Usually this is done using banner ads that are displayed in strategic locations on your blog. The sponsor would give you the appropriate code to place on your website or blog. This type of monetization is somewhat similar to affiliate marketing but the difference is that the blogger is paid per click (PPC) made on the specific banner ad rather than being paid a commission on the sales made in affiliate marketing.

To make your blog sponsorship friendly, you could consider including a page entitled "Sponsors" or "Advertising". On this page you would include some key information such as list prices, acceptable payment options, a short description of your blog demographics and an indication of the type of traffic that you receive on your blog on a monthly or daily basis. Offer at least 3 different package options for sponsors to choose from and make it easy for them to buy sponsorship by including an "order" or "buy" button within the page. This is a very good way to attract sponsorship for your blog. In addition you can consider reaching out to potential sponsors through email letters or by writing a blog post indicating that your blog is available for advertisers to place ads on.

Sponsored Posts are when a sponsor pays you to write blog posts about their particular product or service and to feature that post on your blog. Basically you would write a post giving your own personal review of a particular product or service. Usually the sponsor would send you a sample of the particular product or service for you to try for yourself. Having used the product or service, you would then write a post outlining all the best and worst features of the product or service. The aim is to give an objective view on the product to give readers enough information to make a purchase decision. It is important that the blogger indicates somewhere at the beginning of the post that the post is a sponsored post in order to fulfil FTC regulations (if applicable).

You should decide on the rate to charge for doing sponsored posts. Do your research in this area to ensure that you are not undercharging for your services. Some bloggers have been ripped off by sponsors who paid them little and nothing for their services. Don't be caught in this trap. Do your research and decide how much your services are worth and charge accordingly.

There are several other ways that you can earn money blogging. I have outlined the most popular and the simplest methods to get you started on your way to earning the income that you deserve.

11 GET READY TO MAKE PROFITS FROM YOUR BLOG: A CHECKLIST

Many persons get into blogging to make money. Sure there are many bloggers who blog simply because they love to write and they want to share their point of view or expertise with others. However, many bloggers blog to make money or blog as a means of attracting more of their target market. Given the amazing statistics about the benefits of content marketing through blogging, it is no wonder so many persons flock towards blogging. As a matter of fact, statistics produced by Triblio show that 76% of B2B and B2C businesses rely on blogging as a major part of their content marketing strategy. 68% of consumers prefer custom content that is tailored to their needs and preferences. The more content that is generated, the more inbound traffic your blog or business is able to attract. Blogging also increases engagement, builds customer loyalty, builds brand awareness, establishes the blogger as a thought leader, generates more leads and ultimately results in more sales. The icing on the cake is the fact that blogging is as much as 62% less expensive than traditional outbound marketing. The implication is that if you can find a way to build a great blog that attracts a loyal readership, you will be well on your way to making profits. But is your blog ready to make you profits? Here are 10 things you need to consider:

1. **A List-Building Strategy and System**

You have probably heard the saying that "the money is in the list." This saying is absolutely true. As soon as you decide to go live with your blog, you must implement a system to get the email addresses of prospective customers. By so doing, you are building a database of qualified leads to which you can consistently market your various products or services. These people are considered your warm market once they have shown interest in your offerings by opting in to your mailing list. Instead of hoping that people will find you through search engines, your email list ensures that YOU have the upper hand and that you can contact your prospects with specific and targeted messages on a regular basis. However, it is also important that you automate the system by using auto-responders such as those provided by Aweber or Mailchimp. These services allow you to create a series of emails beforehand and to determine when these emails should be sent out to prospects and in what order. The emails will be sent out automatically at the dates and times that you indicate, freeing you up to complete other necessary tasks. Each time someone opts into your list, they are automatically added to your database in your Aweber or Mailchimp account. Your database is therefore built up over time without much effort on your part except that you need to ensure that you have a steady flow of pre-prepared emails that your selected auto-responder will send out at the appointed time. You can also use this system to send out your regular blog posts to your list of prospects. It will be only a matter of time before you start reaping the financial benefits of your list.

2. **Fresh, relevant content** – The whole purpose of blogging is to provide your readers with useful, up to date information that will help them to achieve their established goals. This means that your blog should always have recently published information that is especially relevant to your target audience. This is a sure way of establishing yourself as a thought leader and building your credibility and brand image. It is important that you establish a publishing schedule and stick to it. An editorial calendar is a useful tool for scheduling blog posts. While it is not necessary to publish every day, it is important to keep in constant and consistent contact with your readers. The frequency of publishing should be based on your particular industry and the needs of your target audience. For example, if you are in the tech industry or the fashion industry, you should be blogging more often to keep your audience updated on quickly changing trends. By so doing, you secure 'top of mind' status in the consciousness of your

readers and they are more likely to think of you if they have a need that your business (or blog) is able to fulfil. Once you have built up a reputation of always publishing valuable and timely content, you are well on your way to creating a loyal following that is very likely to become your loyal customer base.

3. **Professional Design**

If you are blogging for profit, your blog or website should confirm that you are a professional who is running a serious business. This does not mean that you can't use a more casual, conversational tone in your posts. It just means that your blog should exude an air of professionalism and should be well-designed and not look amateurish. Consider getting your blog designed by a professional or using a professionally built, premium theme if you want to do-it-yourself, like I did. I would advise that you stay away from free themes if you can afford to since they tend to have limited features and may be unresponsive (not able to be viewed on mobile devices). With more and more people using mobile devices including a multitude of smartphones and tablets, you wouldn't want to miss out on any market share by having a theme that is not responsive. However, there are some very good free themes available. The key is to find a good free theme or to opt for a premium theme. You may also opt to have your theme custom designed. These cost more, however.

Carefully consider which platform your blog is built on. WordPress is still the most popular and effective platform and is trusted by large, established corporations such as CNN. This is not to imply that other platforms such as Blogger, Weebly, or Tumblr are not good choices. It is just that WordPress has built a reputation as a more professional platform, while the other platforms may be better suited to building a blog that is not necessarily focused on making profits. Your blog should have a good navigation system so that readers can easily find the information that they want. The menus should be prominent as well as the search area. The fonts used should be easy to read and the graphics should be appropriate for your audience needs.

4. **Social Media Connections**

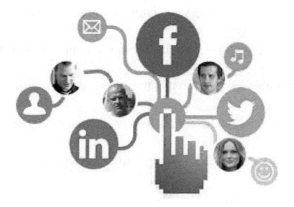

Whether you like it or not, social media is a must if you want to make profits from your blog. It is imperative that you establish and build social media accounts on which your readers and prospects can engage with you outside of your blog. Social media is the equivalent of networking in the real world. It is getting to know others, meeting others in your field, engaging with influencers and getting to know your audience on a more personal level. It is building a discussion around topics of interest and learning what your audience wants by keeping your ears close to the ground. You can gain valuable insight through your social media interactions. However, instead of just using social media as a means of spreading your blog posts, use it as an engagement tool where you listen as much as you 'speak'. Bear in mind that your social media accounts also need to be up-to-date and your posts should be recent and relevant. It does not look professional to have a twitter account that has the last tweet dated 4 months ago. Ensure that all social media accounts are maintained just as well as your blog content. Otherwise, you are compromising on your profit-making ability. Tools like those offered by Hootsuite help you to automatically schedule posts to over 100 social media accounts. This way, your accounts are kept fresh and updated and you don't have to spend hours posting to separate social media accounts.

5. **A profit strategy** – If you want to make profit from your blog, you must have a strategy for earning that profit. The most successful businesses start with a business plan that guides all their major decisions. Similarly, you should establish a vision for your blog and decide upon a mission. Where do you see yourself one (1) year down the line and what will you do daily to ensure that you meet those goals? How exactly will you make a profit? These are questions that you need to answer before going live with your blog. If you are a blogger that is blogging for profit you need to decide which monetization techniques you will use. Will you be doing affiliate marketing, selling your own products and services, running a paid membership or subscription site or using other means of monetization? For businesses using their blog to drive traffic, the decision about how to move customers from content to purchase needs to be addressed. Will you blog about your latest products and services and invite customers in store to take advantage of your offerings? Or will you offer those products or services

online? How many products do you need to sell or how many jobs do you need to complete to make a profit from your blog? How will you get traffic to your blog? While having a blog is all well and good, if nobody knows about it, or if nobody is reading it, all your efforts would have been in vain. Establishing realistic expectations and making realistic plans is an important part of being ready to make a profit from your blog.

6. **A Solid Marketing Plan** – A blog will not market itself. It takes a considerable amount of effort to establish an online presence and deciding beforehand how you will do this will make your job much easier and more effective. Just like any other business venture, no matter how great the offering, if nobody knows about it, you will not meet your income and profit goals. Questions that needs to be answered include how much money will you allocate to marketing your blog or business? And how will that budget be spent? Will you engage in paid advertising, sponsored social media marketing and how much will you spend and on which platforms? Will you advertise mostly on

Facebook, Twitter or through Google Adwords? Marketing is an area that too many bloggers fail to do effectively. While blogging is about writing, without effective marketing skills, your attempts at making blog profits will be ineffective. If you are a new blogger who cannot afford to pay much for marketing services, you should invest in learning as much as you can about marketing your blog yourself. There is a lot of free information available on Youtube and elsewhere on the internet about how to market your blog effectively. My blog at http://www.wealthcreateonline.com has lots of valuable, free information about the business of blogging for profit. Make sure that you find out how to market yourself effectively and implement the relevant marketing strategy.

7. **A Reliable and Appropriate Computer/Laptop** – Your computer or laptop will be the main asset that will help you to earn an income and generate a profit from your blog. A computer that is constantly freezing up because of insufficient memory or that is being affected by viruses will

hamper your ability to be productive. Ensure that your computer can handle all the processing and storage needs that you have. In addition, your internet service, and your hosting service should be reliable. Invest in a good antivirus program and make sure that your information is sufficiently protected from hackers. McAfee is a great antivirus software that you can explore. The proper tools are necessary for you to be successful at blogging and must be in tip top condition so that you can make maximum profits from your blogging efforts.

8. **Long-term commitment** – Contrary to popular belief, a blog is not a way to get rich quickly. In fact, to become a successful blogger, you need to be prepared to invest a good amount of time in the business before you start making profits. While the start-up costs are minimal compared to traditional brick and mortar businesses, it will still take time for you to build a following and to have a steady amount of organic traffic. This means that you need to commit upfront to doing what is necessary to get your

blog to that place where it becomes a lean, mean profit-making machine. There is no standard time period for you to start making a profit and it depends a lot on your efforts and how effectively you run your blog. If you plan on having a profitable blog, be prepared to be in it for the long haul. Commit to doing the right things every day to take you further along the journey of profitmaking. If you give up easily or are easily discouraged, blogging may not be your best bet. A long-term mind-set is necessary.

9. **Be Prepared to Fail, to Accept Criticism and Rejection** – The hard truth is that not everybody will be pleased with your content and your products and services. Not everybody will sign up for your mailing list or your newsletter or your blog posts and you will have subscribers who will unsubscribe. Your points of view may be challenged and you may attract some haters. Be prepared to stand behind your convictions and decisions and to back up your arguments. Your methods will not please everyone and you need to accept this as a natural part of business. It is important that you don't take things personally. Instead

of focusing on the criticisms, focus instead on what you can learn in the process and what you may be doing that could be done more effectively. Choose your battles well. Some battles are just not worth it. The important thing is that you learn in the process.

10. **Privacy Policy and Terms of Service** – Just like any other business, the legal aspects must be sorted out up front. It is important that you create and publish both a privacy policy as well as "Terms of Service" which will outline the rules and terms of using your blog or website from the perspective of your readers. In these documents, you will let visitors know what your privacy policy is such as whether you use cookies on your site, whether information that they supply will be shared with third parties etc. Users want to feel assured that the information that they share with you is safe and not misused. These documents also outline to users exactly what they agree to by doing business with you and using the information, products or services offered from your website. An additional incentive to publishing your terms and conditions is that

Google uses it as an indication that your site is authentic and not a spam site. It doesn't have to be expensive to get these documents drafted. There are legal professionals on Fiverr that offer this service for as little as $5.

So are you ready to get wealthy from your blog? Follow this checklist and you'll be well on your way to earning a decent online income.

"You don't have to be great to get started but you have to get started to be great" – Les Brown.

12 HOW TO NOT LOOK LIKE A NEWBIE BLOGGER

You may be a newbie blogger but the whole world doesn't have to know that. It's about faking it until you make it. There are several things that you can do to give your blog a professional appearance and the impression that you know what you are doing. This is essential to building a following and in establishing your blog as an authority blog and later on in establishing yourself as an influencer or authority blogger. Bear in mind however, that becoming an influencer and building a solid following is going to take both time and effort. It won't happen overnight. The tips I am about to share with you will give you a jump start and considerably shorten your learning curve as a blogger. There are certain things that new bloggers do or forget to do that give away the fact that they are just beginning. I will show you how to avoid falling into that trap. Here are the things you need to do to give your blog a professional look and to give your visitors an excellent browsing experience.

Remove the "Hello World" Post

I can't tell you the number of times I have seen newbie bloggers forget to remove the "Hello World" post from their blogs. This is the template that comes standard with most WordPress free themes and absolutely must be replaced by your own post. This standard post usually looks something like this:

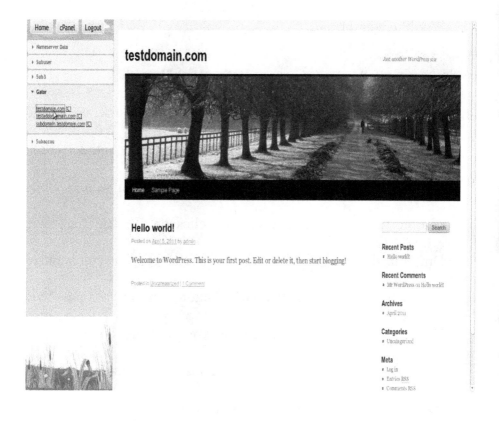

I remember seeing a newbie blogger post a link to his blog on LinkedIn with the "Hello World" post still intact on his blog. That was a dead giveaway that he was new to blogging and that he really did not know much about blogging. Do yourself a favour and edit the post or delete it completely and replace it with your own post. You can edit the post by following these steps from the WordPress dashboard:

>Post >All Posts >Click on "Hello World" > Click in the Title box, delete the words "Hello World" and replace them with the Title of your new post. Next click in the body box and delete the existing text. Replace those words with your own words. When you are through entering your post, click on "Update" or "Save Draft" in the sidebar. Make any other changes that you want to make and then click the "Publish" button to make your post live. However, please check to ensure that your post has all the elements that make it worthy of publication such as proper grammar, proper spelling, at least one image, correct font size etc.

WordPress Dashboard

Change the Header Image

Next, you need to change the Header Image. Most WordPress themes come with a standard header image but you have the option of changing this image and replacing it with your own. Your header should be relevant to your blog and must reflect what your blog is all about. For example, if you are a fashion blogger, you could use a header image of people dressed in fashionable clothing. Just choose something appropriate and use it. The best thing would be to get a custom header designed. This may be done cheaply by using the services of a graphic designer at Fiverr.com. You can get a professionally designed header banner on Fiverr for as little as $5. After you have decided on what to use for your new header, you need to go ahead and upload it to your blog or website. Here are the steps for uploading your new header.

Go to your Dashboard. Scroll down and click on Appearance > Header > Header Image > Add New Image > Upload Files > Select File > Select and Crop.

Depending on the theme you are using you may need to go to Appearance > Customize > Header etc. instead of going directly to Header from the Appearance menu. Ensure that your image dimensions fit comfortably within the header area and that it looks great with the theme that you are using. If everything looks great then you have done well. Your brand new header will help you to exude 'professionalism.'

Upload a Site Icon/Favicon

Your website icon or blog icon is the little icon that you see in the top left hand corner of the tab that your site is loaded up to. It may be the same image as your logo or you may choose to use a different icon. Here are some examples of site icons for Twitter, WordPress and Google websites:

If you don't change your site icon, it will appear as the standard WordPress blog site icon which looks like the WordPress.com site icon illustrated above or like a small blue, checkered box as illustrated below:

Although it's not a hard and fast 'rule' per se, Newbie bloggers are the ones who normally continue to use the standard WordPress icons. If you don't want to be forever perceived as a newbie blogger, it is best if you upload your own customized site icon. The steps for doing so from the WordPress dashboard are as follows:

Settings > General > Site Icon > Update Site Icon

13 HOW TO LET OTHERS KNOW ABOUT YOUR BLOG –

FREE TRAFFIC

An important aspect of blogging for profit is getting people to purchase something as a result of being influenced by your blog content. But no one can buy something that they don't know anything about. Apart from writing excellent content, you must get that content in front of your target market. Otherwise, you will only be speaking to yourself and your message would only be making an impact on you. At the end of the day, if there is no traffic coming to your blog, you won't be able to make any money from your blogging efforts. As a new blogger, you may wonder how to get others to learn about your blog and where to find an audience. There are many sources of free traffic and I will now elaborate on a few of them.

Persons researching online

Every second, there are 40,000 searches conducted on Google! This means that everyday there are more than 3.5 billion searches conducted by people searching online for something! Within this number is your niche market. The people that you are targeting are a subset of those 3.5 billion people that are searching on Google for something. If the content that you have generated on your blog contains keywords that are equal to, similar to or closely related to the keyword searches made by your target market, Google's search engines may bring up your blog posts in their search results. If the people conducting these keyword searches click on your blog article's URL, they will be taken to your blog where they can read the entire article. If your content satisfies their query, it is likely that they will read more of your blog for further information. They may even find products or services on your blog that are suitable for meeting their needs and they may make purchases from your blog. Bear in mind also that other search engines such as Yahoo! or Bing also receive lots of keyword searches on a daily basis. Your target market could be among this group as well. Therefore search engines are a great source of free traffic for you. However, you must learn to write your content so that it is optimized for the search engines. The WordPress SEO plugin will help you greatly to generate SEO optimized content. If done correctly, this has the potential to send significant amounts of traffic to your blog.

Social Media Platforms

Social media platforms may be an excellent sources of free traffic for your blog. It is therefore important that you operate social media accounts on the major social media platforms such as Facebook, Twitter, LinkedIn, Instagram, Pinterest, Google Plus, Youtube etc. I recommend that you create a separate fan page on Facebook if that is one of the platforms that you decide to use. It is not mandatory that you have an account on each platform but choose a few and use them to introduce your blog to others. You can do this by posting links to your blog articles on this platforms where acceptable. You may set up your blog to utilize the publicize function that allows you to connect your selected social media accounts to your blog. Whenever you publish a blog post, it will automatically be shared on your social media platforms. To set this up go to your dashboard and click on Settings > Sharing > You will end up on the Publicize page. Press the connect button and give the necessary permission to WordPress to connect your blog to these accounts. You should join as many groups as you can on Facebook, LinkedIn, Google Plus etc. When posting your links however, be careful to avoid spamming. Also, remember that these are social media platforms and so apart from sharing your content, you should also be actively engaging in conversation with other group members, commenting on their posts, sharing some of their content with your audience, asking relevant questions etc. This process may be time consuming but you will find that it is well worth it when you see that it sends traffic to your blog. There are services such as those offered by Hootsuite that will help you in managing the posting on these platforms.

Following and Interacting with other Bloggers

There are several other bloggers in the blogosphere who are interested in connecting with you, reading your content, sharing your content, following your blog, commenting on your blog posts and just making a connection. Use this fact to your advantage by reaching out to other bloggers, especially those who may have a similar audience to yours. By following or subscribing to their blogs, some will return the favour and follow your blog as well. Also make an effort to read the blogs of others and to make value-added comments where appropriate. Avoid simply saying things like "great post". Make an effort to say something meaningful if something on their blog sparks your interest or gets your attention.

Other persons who are reading those blogs may like your comment, click on your gravatar and end up on your own blog. I personally have received a good amount of traffic from doing this. Be certain to make your gravatar clickable however. You should have set this up earlier when you had established your gravatar profile. This method of traffic generation is especially useful when you comment on blogs that already receive a good amount of traffic. You can find this out by checking their Alexa rank at Alexa.com. The lower the rank, the more traffic that blog receives.

Participating in Forums and Group Discussions

Take the opportunity to take part in group forums and discussions. This will allow people to get to know you and it will also give you the chance to get to know others and to learn from them. By participating you are also inviting attention to yourself and by conducting intelligent and meaningful conversations, you will pique the interests of others. If you can, offer solutions to problems that people may be having and also feel free to ask relevant questions to keep the conversation going.

Later on in your blog journey, you can also get traffic to your blog by guest posting on other blogs. However, that method is for more advanced bloggers who have more experience blogging. There are several other methods but these alone should be able to help you generate a good amount of traffic as you start.

If you follow all these steps, you will be well on your way to earning a good income as a blogger. Thanks so much for purchasing and reading my book. Please help me to get this valuable resource out to more people by leaving a review on Amazon. Thanks so much!

14 GLOSSARY

Administrator:

The person or persons who are responsible for posting information to your blog such as new articles, new updates, responding to comments and other feedback, clearing the blog of spam etc. In other words, this person is responsible for keeping the blog updated and fresh. In many cases, you are the administrator. However, you can hire someone to administer on your behalf.

Affiliate:

An affiliate is someone who is connected to someone else through business for the purpose of increasing sales. For example, let's use Amazon to illustrate this principle. Amazon wants to expand its market so it decides to give bloggers the right to sell stuff on Amazon's behalf by allowing bloggers to advertise Amazon's products on their blogs. Let's say you have a blog that deals with fashion. Persons visit your site and see an advertisement about a fashion item. They click on the ad and as a result, they end up purchasing a fashion item that you are advertising on Amazon's behalf. As a reward, Amazon pays you a commission on the purchase since the sale originated through your blog site. You are considered to be an **affiliate** and what you are doing is called affiliate marketing. Several established businesses use affiliates to increase sales. Clickbank is another popular website that markets through its vast network of affiliates.

Analytics:

This is statistical information that helps you with decision making. The information helps you to measure the effectiveness of your marketing efforts and all online activities. If you run an ad on your Facebook page, you want to know how well the ad has performed so you can decide to continue to use it or to use it as a reference point for other ads in the future. Depending on the goal of your ad, you can view information such as the number of clicks on the ad, the number of views of that ad, the number and volume of purchases that those ads influenced etc. For your blog, if you use WordPress, you have the ability to see how many clicks you get to the site, the origin of the referral link to your blog, the search terms that were used to find your site, the number of views that a particular post or page gets, the number of clicks on links in your blog post and so on. If you advertise on Google, Google Analytics is a useful tool that tells you all about the results of your online activities. WordPress also gives its bloggers useful analytics such as the number of views your blog posts get, the number of visitors to your website/blog, the country where your visitors come from, the other pages that were viewed on your blog etc. These are very useful points of information that allow you to see the effects of your efforts in a graphical way.

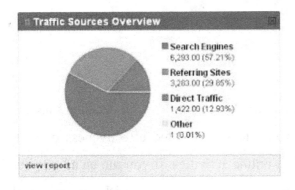

Akismet :

Akismet is a service that WordPress offers to identify and prevent comment spam. You should activate this handy plugin on your blog to prevent your blog being overwhelmed by lots of unwelcome spam. Once a comment has two or more links within it, Akismet identifies it as spam and automatically sends it to a spam folder and therefore prevents it from automatically being displayed on your site. You now have the option of checking the comment yourself and deciding whether it is spam or not and whether you want it to appear in your blog comments or discarded.

Akismet API key:

This is a string of characters that is used to register akismet for your blog site. Once you get an akismet API key, you can set up the akismet plugin on your blog site.

Alexa Ranking: Alexa is the name of an Amazon affiliated organization that ranks all websites and blogs according to the amount of traffic that the site generates over a period of time and essentially is an estimate of the site's popularity. The global rank is calculated using a combination of average daily visitors to the site, and the number of page views over the last 3 months. A site may also be ranked in a specific country and this is an estimate of the site's popularity in that specific country. The most popular site (which is Google.com) has an Alexa rank of 1. The more popular the site, the lower the rank value. For example, a site with a rank of 45,123 is doing better than a site with a rank of 76,356. As a blogger, your Alexa rank is going to be an important measure of your popularity and of your impact.

Alt text:

Alt is an abbreviation for alternative. So 'alt text' means alternative text and it is required for images that cannot be read by certain text browsers. Whenever you put an image into your blog post, you are required to provide an alt text for that image. This text allows your blog site to be easily picked up by search engines like Google or Yahoo or Bing. For images that have text on them, the alt text should be the same as the text contained in the image itself. For example the alt text for the following image should be 'best free blogging websites'.

For images that don't have text, you should use text that closely describes the image being displayed. It is a good idea to keep the alt text short – no more than 15 words and it is also a good idea to use some of your SEO keywords as the alt text. Don't worry that you may not know what SEO or keyword mean, simply find those meanings in this handy guide and read on….Everything is all here for you my lovely wannabes! Soon you will be a pro!

Amazon: So you may be totally new to this blogging or online business thing and may have never even heard of Amazon before. Well, Amazon is the largest online retailer in the world. They carry the greatest range of books available in both print and digital (e-book) form. In additional Amazon carries a whole other range of electronics and music and jewellery, beauty products and just about anything that you could buy in a regular retail store. Amazon has done amazing things by allowing ordinary writers to self-publish their books all in a few simple steps.

Aweber: Aweber is an email marketing service that allows you to easily manage your email marketing campaigns through the use of autoresponders, sign-up forms and so on.

Backlink:

A backlink is a link that links back to your blog. For example, let's say that you write an excellent blog post about gourmet meals. Sharon, who is also a blogger who writes about food, writes an article on her blog about food. Sharon likes your article so much that within her own article, she creates a link that links your original blog post to her blog. By doing this Sharon hopes to capitalize on the traffic that your site gets. Once Sharon links to your site, within the comments section on your blog post, you will see a link entitled "links to your post". If a visitor to your site clicks on that link, they will be taken to Sharon's blog post. As a result, your site is essentially driving traffic to Sharon's blog. If you are the one who creates the backlink, you are driving traffic back to your own blog. The more backlinks that link to your blog site, the higher your blog will rank in a Google or other search engine search. This means that each time someone searches for keywords that are associated with your blog, the more likely it is that your blog will show up on the first few pages of Google thereby earning your blog site more clicks and hopefully more sales. Many bloggers believe that backlinks are essential for driving traffic to your blog site. Back links can also come through directories, press releases, social network profiles, social bookmarks and related sites.

Backup:

It is possible for information that you have posted to your blog to be lost whenever your blog host, for example, carries out maintenance on all the sites that it serves or something happens to corrupt the information on your blog. To prevent this from happening, you need to backup your blog by 'saving' all the information on the site before the scheduled maintenance takes place in order to prevent loss of essential information. I learned this the hard way when I just started my blog and did not backup my site when I received notification from my website host about an upcoming maintenance. Suffice it to say that I was not happy when I discovered that several pieces of valuable information had been lost and there was no way to recover that information. Well guess who always backups now? If you learn nothing else, please learn this. Backup is essential. Do it often. You will save yourself a lot of heartache. You also need to back up your site before you install upgrades and some plugins.

Banner ad:

There are several types of advertisements on the internet. A banner ad is a special type of advertisement usually in the form of an image with text that is usually rectangular in shape and that appears somewhere on the internet (other sites apart from your blog) to attract visitors to click. They may appear either at the top, at the bottom or to the sides of a website and when clicked, they lead visitors to your website or blog. Here is an example of a banner ad.:

Black hat SEO technique:

A Black hat SEO technique is a technique in which aggressive SEO strategies are utilized to capitalize on search engines instead of on actual human traffic. Many times, SEO guidelines are ignored in order to manipulate the system. It may involve things such as keyword stuffing, doorway pages and page swapping. Black hat SEO techniques should be avoided if you want to establish a reputable blog.

Factor	White Hat	Black Hat
On-page Factor	Properly research and craft Title, Meta tags, & Content according to web page, industry, relevance.	Stuff & spam keywords into the on-page contents to fool the search engine spiders & improve ranking.
Links	Link Bait: Getting linked because of quality content.	Link Farm: Exchange links to improve ranking. Hiding links on your site.
Content	Write content in which the keyword density is optimally maintained, which makes visitors read your content.	Stuff keywords in your content that makes your visitors a pain to read your content.

Blog:

A blog is the short name for a weblog. It is essentially a personal website that is used to maintain a 'log' of anything that the creator desires such as articles about fashion, cars, health, or any other subject. The intention is to engage an audience to read the content that is posted to establish oneself as an expert in a certain area. It is actually a website but it is used to express and share opinions and ideas with a targeted audience rather than a commercialized portal through which online purchases are facilitated. Even though online purchases can be done through blogs also, the main focus of blogs is to share valuable content with readers. A **blogger** is someone who operates a blog.

Bluehost:

Bluehost is the name of a popular website hosting service. A website needs to be hosted in order for it to be accessible to anyone. A website may be created but unless it is hosted, it will not be viewable to anyone except the creator. All the information that you create on your blog is saved and generated for publishing on Bluehost servers (if Bluehost is your selected hosting service).

Best Hosting For Wordpress Bloggers

Bounce rate:

This is the rate at which visitors to your site leave after viewing only one page on your blog or website. Ideally, you don't want your bounce rate to be high because you want your visitors to be engaged with your content. Engaged visitors are more likely to return to the site and are more likely to become loyal paying customers or clients or subscribers to your blog. You want visitors to visit more than one page on your blog and to engage by liking, commenting, sharing etc.

BAD LANDING PAGES

Call To Action (CTA):

This is an invitation to an online user to do an action such as to subscribe to your blog, or to follow your blog, or to sign up for your weekly newsletters, or to buy something etc. It is usually in the form of a button or banner with an accompanying appeal to act. See examples here:

Campaign:

An online marketing campaign is a carefully crafted series of marketing messages with a specific aim in mind. The aim may be to inform, educate, demonstrate how a product works, to capture qualified leads, to recruit committed readers to your site, to advise readers about a new product that you have launched etc. Effective marketing campaigns should result in the accomplishment of the campaign goals. For example, you may create a campaign to get 500 likes to your facebook page over a 2 day period. At the end of the campaign, if you have achieved your goal, your campaign would be considered as successful.

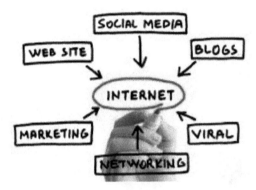

Click Through Rate:

The click through rate is the rate at which people who are browsing click on a link to your blog site via an ad or link. It is determined by dividing the number of clicks by the number of impressions (number of times your ad is shown). The higher the number of clicks, the higher is the click through rate. The click through rate is a measure of the effectiveness of your ads and is a useful guide when determining what is effective and what is not. It also helps to determine the effectiveness of your keywords.

$$\frac{5 \text{ clicks}}{100 \text{ Impressions}} = 5\% \text{ CTR}$$

36% of Google users will click on the first result*

Content:

As the name suggests, the content is whatever is contained on the blog. It usually takes the form of articles that should be full of very valuable information that readers want to read. Content is important because it is what determines whether people will take your information seriously and act upon the advice or recommendations that you may give.

Cookie: A cookie is a small amount of information that is collected through an internet user's web browser which is used to identify a web user and is often used to track browsing patterns in order to create a customized browsing experience for the user. Cookies can save such things as login details after permission is received from the internet user to do so. Based on the user's browsing patterns, cookies help users to navigate to customized pages based on their prior browsing patterns.

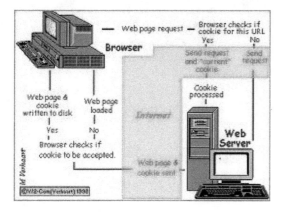

Conversion:

The rate at which clicks on an ad or on a link result in a purchase or any other desired action is known as the conversion rate. For example, let's say that 100 people click on your ad and of the 100 clicks, 5 people end up buying the product being advertised. The conversion rate in this case would be 5/100 = 5%.

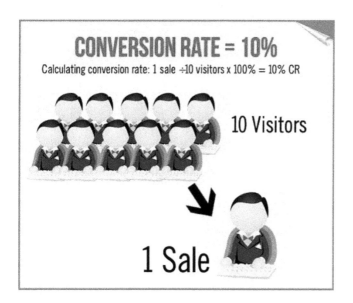

Cpanel:

Cpanel is the short name for control panel. This is a graphical interface on the host server from where files and other processes such as backups for your blog site can be managed.

CSS Code:

This is a programming code used to design a website and also to create HTML templates. CSS is short for Cascading Style Sheet. This code is used to format the look of a website including the fonts, the colors, the basic layout etc. The CSS code makes websites easier to develop.

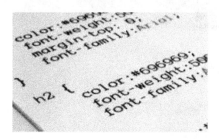

Dashboard:

Ok think of your car's dashboard. This is where all the controls are located such as the steering wheel, the glove compartment, the air conditioning, the stereo etc. A blog has a similar panel where all the controls for you to manage your blog are located. This is where you do things like create posts to your blog, add pages, add images, alter the look of your blog, change your blog theme and so on. In other words, the dashboard is similar to your back office where all the work takes place to give your blog the professional, finished look that you want it to have. Below is an example of a WordPress dashboard.

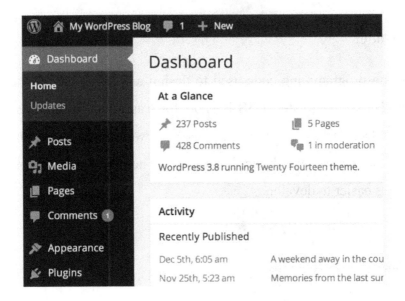

Domain:

This is the part of a web address that identifies the owner of that particular website. For example, the following web pages all have the same domain (name):

www.CurryKing.com/take-out

www.CurryKing.com/dine-in

www.CurryKing.com/home

www.CurryKing.com/About

The domain would be CurryKing. The information after the .com/ simply indicates the name of a particular page or location on the CurryKing website.

Download:

This means to pull information from the internet. When you do a search on Google for example, when the search results are shown, you would click on a link and the information that you need would be 'downloaded' or opened for your viewing.

Dropbox:

A dropbox is a location on the internet where files can be uploaded for sharing purposes. Let's say I am a part of a book club and each member of the book club agrees to do a book review of another member's book each week. All members of the group want to see each review so a space is created online where each member can go and post their review. Each member now has the ability to visit that location and view all the review files that have been uploaded. Dropbox.com offers such a service. This service provides an alternative to sending emails to multiple parties.

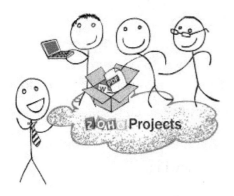

Doorway page:

A doorway page is a webpage that is created to 'trick' search engines into ranking it highly for

the purpose of leading visitors to another page that usually has nothing to do with the keyword that was searched. These pages are usually used in black hat SEO techniques. You should refrain from using these techniques if you intend to create a good reputation for yourself and your blog. In the online world, using doorway pages can be considered as unethical behavior.

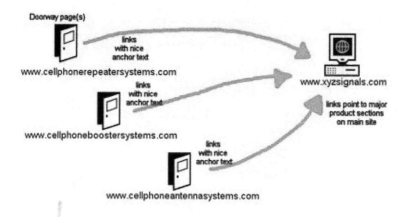

Ebook:

This is the shortened form of electronic book. If you are reading this on a kindle device or other electronic device, or even on your regular laptop or PC you are reading an ebook. Ebooks are great alternatives to paper based books that are relatively more costly to print and may be difficult to carry around because of the size and the weight.

Email marketing:

This is, as the name suggests, using emails as the means of carrying out an online marketing campaign.

Email marketing is important for keeping your target audience engaged and is useful for getting your messages to your target market directly. Some popular email marketing tools are provided by companies such as Aweber and Mailchimp. My personal favorite is Aweber because it is easy to use and has lots of very useful features.

Encryption:

Encoding messages in such a way that only authorized readers are able to read it. Encryption is usually used on websites where products are sold and buyers may be required to input their credit card information online in order to purchase those products. The encryption prevents identity theft as well as the stealing of credit card and other personal information.

Follow:

This is a popular social media jargon used on platforms such as Twitter and Facebook and means that fans are following up on your posts or other content that you publish.

Font:

A font is a style of shaping letters. For example, this book is written in the Times New Roman font and the letters are shaped a certain way. It is similar to a type of handwriting. Everyone's handwriting is different because we shape our letters differently. If the book were written in the Arial font, the letters would be shaped differently. Here are some examples:

Arial

Times New Roman

Metro

Signature

Old English

Vladimir Script

Groups:

A group is a set of persons with similar interests coming together in an online forum to accomplish certain tasks such as to hold a discussion or to share ideas and opinions etc. If you are a parent for example, you may be eligible to join groups whose purpose is to share parenting stories. Facebook and LinkedIn give you the option of joining interest groups.

Gravatar:

Gravatar is short for Globally Recognized Avatar and as the name suggests, it is an avatar that is used like an online ID. It is normally an image that appears next to your name in your online avatar. It follows you across the web and appears whenever you post comments etc online. Here are some examples of default gravatars. One of these will appear next to your name instead of your photo if you haven't uploaded a photograph to your gravatar profile.

Grey hat SEO technique:

As the name suggests, grey hat SEO (search engine optimization) is somewhere between white hat techniques and black hat techniques. White hat techniques are recommended and black hat techniques are not recommended. Grey hat techniques are only recommended when done by a professional who does not abuse the system. Grey hat techniques include things such as cloaking, purchasing old domains, duplicating content, link buying, social media automation and the purchasing of followers.

Google Adsense:

This is a free, flexible form of advertising on the Google platform that allows you to earn money when surfers click on an ad that you allow to be published on your website or blog.

Google Adwords:

Google allows you to place your ads next to related Google search results using your Google Adwords account. These ads appear in the pink boxes at the top of google search results.

Hashtag:

This is the "#" sign which is placed before a word or a string of words to indicate the topic of discussion. It is used to discuss trending topics or to create buzz around certain events or occasions. The hashtag is a way for people to categorize, find and join conversations on a particular topic. The hashtag is a popular symbol used on Twitter. It is also being used increasingly on Facebook.

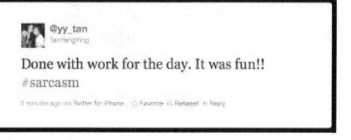

Header:

This is an image (it may contain text as well) that usually appears at the top of a webpage, running horizontally from left to right. It tells what the page or website is all about.

H1 Tag

This is short for header tag 1 and it is usually the title of a post and it usually appears in bigger and bolder font than the body of the post itself. It usually stands out from the other text because of its size. Header tags usually range from H1 to H4 with H1 being the largest and boldest and H4 being the smallest. Tags are used for SEO so that search engines can easily match them to appropriate searches.

Hootsuite: Hootsuite is an online media tool that allows you to effectively manage your social media marketing by enabling users to schedule the publishing of social posts to the various social media platforms. It can be very time-consuming to manage your social media messages since there are so many social media platforms that you may need to consider. Hootsuite allows you to create one post that you can schedule to send out to all your social media accounts at specified times. Click the Hootsuite image below to learn more about Hootsuite:

Hosting:

This is the service that allows your website to be "live" and accessible for internet users. Bluehost and Hostgator are examples of hosting services.

HTML code:

This is the programming code that is used to construct a website. It is a special type of 'language' that programmers use.

```
<html>
<head>
 <title>This is Jennifer's test web page</title>
</head>
<body>
 <h1>Jennifer's test web page</h1>
  <p>This is a web page by Jennifer that she did for CS8</p>
</body>
</html>
```

Impression:

This is the number of times an online advertisement is seen. It often takes into consideration the number of times an ad is clicked or the number of times an ad is scrolled pass in a newsfeed or rss feed.

Javascript:

Javascript is a special type of computer programming language that is used especially in controlling browsers.

Keyword:

A phrase or string of words that browsers type into search engines to find relevant information on the web. Note that a keyword is not actually a word, but is really a phrase. Keywords are similar to tags but tags are usually one word and keywords are strings of words. An example of a keyword is "New York fashion designers" and a related tag could be "fashion". Keywords are very important in driving traffic to your website and should be selected carefully when creating web content.

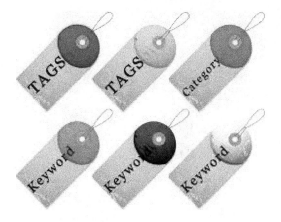

Kindle:

A Kindle is an electronic reader that allows users to download ebooks and other electronic information. Kindle is actually the brand name for the ereader offered by Amazon.

Landing Page:

A landing page is a special page on a website or blog that a visitor is directed to when he clicks on a particular link. Landing pages are used for either lead generation or click through. The landing page normally prompts the user to supply their email address in order to have full access to the underlying content. Landing page is another word for squeeze page or capture page.

Lead:

A lead is a prospect that has the authority to purchase a product or service. A lead is normally defined by a name and contact information.

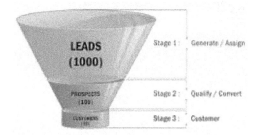

Link:

A link is really the short form of hyperlink and is a connection that takes an online user from one location on the web to another. It is normally identified by blue underlining. Whenever you are online and you see a string of words underlined in blue, it means that you can point and click on those words and you will be taken to another destination on the web. A link is different from a url in that it doesn't have the "http:www" before it. Usually you are taken to another website or to a blog or to a landing page.

Like:

A 'like' is a way of communicating to another user that the content (in whatever form it is) that is being viewed is appreciated and enjoyed. Users usually click the 'like' button to share their feelings about an online post whether it is an article, a blog post, a comment, a photograph, a link....whatever it is. The icon for "like" is usually a "thumbs up" and the more "thumbs up" there are, the more the subject is liked. A "thumbs down" indicates dislike. Five thumbs up usually indicate "love"!

Login:

A login is the area on a website or blog where the user is prompted to put in their unique credentials usually in the form of a username and a password in order to gain access to the site. This is like the online security guard who requires that you provide your name and your password before you are allowed further access to the information on the other side. The login is intended to distinguish you from other users and is used mainly for security purposes to ensure that your identity is not misrepresented online.

Mail Chimp

Mail chimp is a service offered by the Mailchimp company that allows you to send out mass emails to your subscribers. When your capture page captures your prospects' information, Mailchimp allows you to group each prospect into a particular group so that they can be specifically targeted for certain products or services based on their profile and their subscription details. The service gives you the ability to run email campaigns and to keep in touch will your subscribers or customers through emailing. The program allows you to track the results of various email campaigns.

Media file:

This is a computer file that is either in the form of an image, a pdf document, a video clip or an audio clip. Media file just means that it is not a text file. These files usually have the extensions wav, mp3, png, jpeg, avi indicating the type of media file that it is.

Meta description tag:

This is a type of html tag that provides information about a webpage and allows search engines to decide whether to return that particular page on the results listing of a web search query made by a user. These tags help to ensure that your webpage appears in search results but are only optional. They basically tell the search engine what your webpage is about. If you are serious about driving traffic to your site however, meta descriptions tags are a must since they present an opportunity to engage browsers.

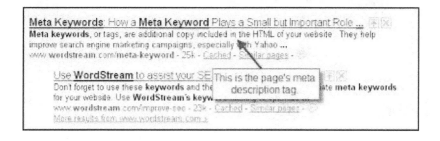

Monetize:

This means offering products and/or services for sale on your blog in order to make money. This can be done in several ways including charging a subscription or membership fee for premium members, selling products or services that you own such as e-books, banner advertising for third parties or selling affiliate products or services.

Online/Offline:

Online simply means on the worldwide web or internet (cyberspace) and offline means in the actual world. If I have an online business and an offline business, it means that I have a business that is accessed through the internet and I also have a regular store in the middle of town from where I sell my merchandise.

On-page SEO / Off-page SEO:

This is the process of formatting your webpage so that it is easily found my search engines. It includes things like including Titles, keywords, meta tags and great content on your webpage. This is different from off page SEO which basically involves the process of creating backlinks to your webpage or blog site.

Opt in:

This is an interface where users have the option of signing up for something or not. Users normally opt in my providing their names and email addresses on a landing page or capture page. This usually allows users access to further information.

Page Ranking:

Page ranking has to do with what page your website ends up on in the various searches on search engines. The aim of most website/blog owners is to have their webpage rank on page 1 of all Google searches for a particular keyword. The higher up your page ranks, the more likely it is that users will click on your link and end up on your blog page or webpage.

Paypal:

Paypal is an online payment service that allows you to send and receive payments online. It is an alternative to using your credit card or debit card directly to make payments or to transfer funds between online accounts.

Pingback:

A pingback is a comment that occurs whenever someone creates a link from their blog back to your blog. For example say I create a blog article about dog snacks. You have a similar blog, see my blog and create an article yourself in which you create a link back to my log. Wordpress would inform you when such an occurrence happens and the comment is called a pingback.

Plagiarism:

Plagiarism occurs whenever someone uses someone else's written work with giving them credit for it by giving the impression that it is their own original work. To avoid plagiarism, always give credit to the writers of content or the creators of information whose work you use in your own writing. Any direct quotes of other writers must be written in quotation marks and must reference the original writer. Attribution should also be given for images.

Plugin:

Plugins are software extensions that increase the functionality of a software program. Several software programs offer optional plugins. For example, Wordpress offers a plugin called WP-ecommerce plugin that allows Wordpress owners to add a shopping cart to their Wordpress site. Plugins are very popular and help users to easily enhance their websites or blogs for optimal reach and performance.

Post:

A post is an online entry such as a comment or an article. Whenever you update your status on Facebook for example or send out a tweet on Twitter, or create an article on your blog, you are making a post.

Profile:

A profile is a combination of features that describe each user uniquely and may include a username, an email address, a password and an avatar and possibly a short description.

Publish:

To publish is to make your content available for public viewing. You can create an article on Wordpress but until you hit the publish button, you will be the only one who can see that article.

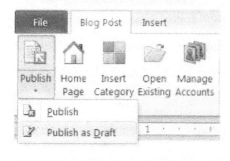

RSS feed:

RSS is an acronym for Rich Site Summary and an RSS feed is an updated form of a series of posts on a blog or online news site that has regularly changing information. Following an RSS feed helps you to avoid the option of subscribing to a blog in order to receive regular updates on the newly published material.

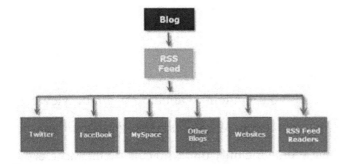

Search Engine: A search engine is a program that is used by online users to find items of interest on the internet by entering keywords. The search engine then returns results based on the keyword search that was carried out. Popular search engines include Google, Yahoo!, and Bing.

Google **Google Search Engine**
82% market share

YAHOO! **Yahoo! Search Engine**
7% market share

bing **Bing Search Engine**
5% market share

Aol. **AOL Search Engine**
0.4% market share

SEO:

SEO is the short form of search engine optimization. Search engine optimization is the process of adjusting your blog or website so that it ranks high for keywords when users do a search online. SEO includes such things like adding meta description tags, adding header tags, adding keywords to your content etc.

Share: This means to broadcast a message so that users connected to you through social networks etc can view the information that you broadcast. This is a powerful way of spreading your message across the internet and is necessary for posts to become viral (be spread quickly across cyberspace). The symbol below is the symbol for share on social networks.

Sidebar: As the name suggests, a sidebar is a horizontal, rectangular strip at the side of a webpage that is usually used to display advertisements, to place widgets and other messages apart from the main message. It can be to the left or to the right of the main message area.

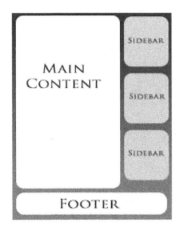

Example of a Sidebar used to display a Youtube video.

Shopping Cart: This is similar to a real life shopping cart and is simply a place where you leave items that you would like to purchase on a website until you are finished shopping and are ready to checkout and pay for those items.

Skyscraper: A skyscraper ad is an advertisement that normally spans the length of a right sidebar. The standard dimensions are 160 x 600 pixels. The Nike ad below is a skyscraper ad.

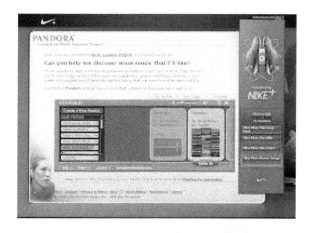

Socialadr: <u>Socialadr</u> is a special software service that helps you to generate traffic to your website. It does this by allowing you to automatically share your content with hundreds of readers as well as to easily allow readers to share that content with their friends and followers on social media platforms. Many persons use Socialadr to create natural backlinks to their website or blog. It is a very valuable software that all bloggers and online marketers should seriously consider using. Click the picture below to learn more about how Socialadr can help drive traffic to your blog or website.

Social Media: Any website or online platform that allows users to share content and to engage in social networking. Popular social media platforms include Facebook, Twitter, LinkedIn, Youtube,

Pinterest, Reddit, Stumbleupon etc.

Spam: Unsolicited messages sent via the internet to large numbers of users for advertising or malicious purposes. Spam is usually sent in the form of email messages or online posts that have little relevance to the recipient or are used to promote irrelevant messages.

Subscriber: A subscriber is someone who opts to receive a regular publication such as a newsletter or a series of emails or blog posts.

Text: Text is anything that consists of letters, numbers or other special symbols and characters. It is anything that is written such as words, sentences, paragraphs etc.

Theme: A WordPress theme is the program that determines how your website or blog looks and the features available to you and to your readers. Different themes support different features. WordPress offers several themes for you to choose from based on your personal preferences and the level of functionality that you desire for your website or blog. Both free and paid themes are available. Studio Press Themes also offers several beautiful, premium WordPress themes from which you can choose. Click the image below to learn more about Studio Press Themes.

Thread: A thread is a series of comments or arguments usually used in online forums. An open thread is where readers are free to discuss or comment on any topic they choose. A comment thread is a series of comments on a certain topic. If one reader replies to the comments of another reader, that is called a threaded comment.

Zach Klein STAFF
6 hours ago:
Jake, can you post a transcript?

⁂THREAD

charliesteadman 5 hours ago
Zach, you write well. You should write a book. :)

Joel
6 hours ago:
Is that line a homage to Donnie Darko?

By the way - that was hilarious!

⁂THREAD

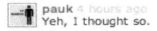
Jakob Lodwick 5 hours ago
It was an homage.

pauk 4 hours ago
Yeh, I thought so.

CHUT UP!

Traffic: In cyberspace, traffic refers to the visitors to a website, blog or other online space. It is the flow of data across the internet.

Tweet: A tweet is a message that is sent on the Twitter social media platform. It is a short message that is limited to 140 characters and is used to communicate on Twitter.

Upload: To transfer a document unto the internet. For eg. If I create a Word document, I can save it on my computer and then 'upload' it to my website where visitors are able to view it online without me having to send it to them via email. Upload simply implies making a document or other type of file available on the internet. While download means to take information from the internet, upload means to send information to the internet.

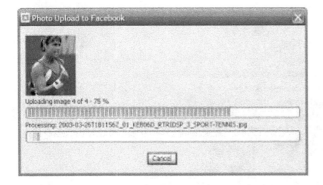

File uploads to the internet

URL: This is the abbreviation for Uniform Resource Locator and it is essentially an online address that tells internet browsers where on the internet to go to find information from a specific address. A url is always preceded by the string http://

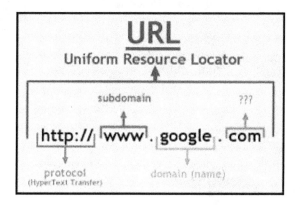

The URL consists of the protocol, the subdomain, the domain and the ending such as .com or .co or .net or .org or .edu. The ending usually indicates the type of organization eg. 'edu' suggests that the organization is an educational institution and 'org' suggests that the organization is not a company but rather, an organization.

Username: A username is a unique name that is used to identify the user on different online platforms. Each username is usually associated with a specific password and together they are used to access online platforms.

Video: A special media type of visual, moving images eg. Youtube video

Views: A view is recorded each time an online user visits a web page. If the visitor clicks on another page in the same website, another view is recorded.

Viral: This term refers to a social media post that becomes popular in a short time and is viewed and shared several times more often than other posts. Viral posts also generate a lot of social "buzz".

10.8K

10K shares
500.000 views
60 links
48 hours

Visitors: The users who visit a website or blog are called visitors.

Month	Unique visitors	Number of visits	Pages	Hits	Bandwidth
Jan 2009	111	227	373	49827	7.73 GB
Feb 2009	91	196	467	1461	310.41 MB
Mar 2009	104	265	534	1452	120.70 MB
Apr 2009	94	202	544	1286	107.28 MB
May 2009	112	280	635	1399	86.91 MB
Jun 2009	108	259	859	1777	88.14 MB
Jul 2009	116	382	796	1703	75.77 MB
Aug 2009	146	463	1249	8829	117.15 MB
Sep 2009	176	544	1174	14878	391.09 MB
Oct 2009	4	4	6	8	34.63 KB
Nov 2009	0	0	0	0	0
Dec 2009	0	0	0	0	0
Total	1062	2822	6637	82620	9.00 GB

Vlog: This is the shortened form of the term "video log" and it is a series of videos that chronicle a certain topic. It is essentially a blog consisting primarily of videos.

Webinar: This is a seminar or a meeting that is hosted on the internet (in virtual space).

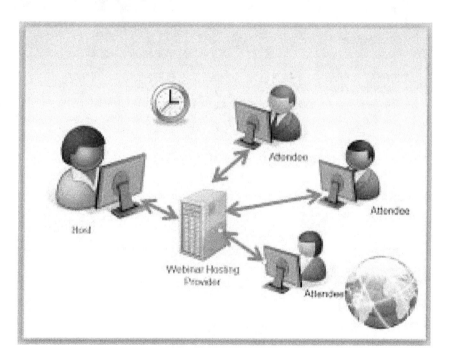

White Hat SEO: This is SEO that follows all search engine rules and policies. It is the correct way to do SEO without being penalized by the search engines such as Google.

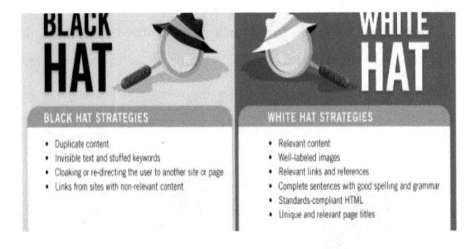

Widget: This is a small software program that can be executed within a website or blog. It usually appears in the form of a clickable link that performs a certain function when clicked. The widget below appears in the sidebar of a blog and when clicked will take the user to the specific blog post that was clicked.

WordPress: This is an online website or blog creation tool. It is also a content management system (CMS). WordPress is the most powerful CMS available.

Youtube: A social media platform that allows for the sharing of videos between users.

15 LEAVE A REVIEW ON AMAZON

Congratulations on taking this step towards realizing your dreams of earning money as a blogger! If you have followed the advice offered in this book, you will achieve success if you are diligent, committed and determined to succeed. If this book has helped you in any way, please help me out by leaving a review on Amazon. See you in the blogosphere!

16 ABOUT THE AUTHOR

Keesha Metcalfe is a serial blogger, Freelance Writer and avid Researcher. She formerly spent several years in the corporate world as a manager within various financial institutions. Today she spends her days blogging and researching on business topics and other areas of interest; having replaced her corporate income with her online income. She is happily married and is the mother of three sons.

Feel free to visit her blog at http://www.wealthcreateonline.com